SCHOLASTIC
ATLAS
OF THE
UNITED
STATES

SCHOLASTIC
ATLAS
OF THE
UNITED
STATES

David Rubel

An Agincourt Press Book

*To Abraham Rosman and Robert Schmeling, on their seventieth
and eightieth years, respectively*

Copy Editor: Ron Boudreau
Proofreader: Laura Jorstad

Art Direction and Production: Oxygen Design
Interior Design, Maps, Illustrations: Sherry Williams, Tilman Reitzle
Image Research: Deborah Goodsite, Julia Rubel
Cover design: Peter Koblish, Nancy Sabato

Special thanks are due Marshall Creighton and Dan Henke of the United States Geological
Survey, Bob Sann, Tracie Cayford of the Utah Travel Council, Amy Hastert of the Wisconsin
Department of Tourism, Jay Hammond of the Kentucky Department of Surface Mining, and
Chris Walker of the *Emporia Gazette.*

For photo credits, see p. 144.

Library of Congress Cataloging-in-Publication Data
Rubel, David.
Scholastic atlas of the United States/by David Rubel.
p. cm.—(Scholastic Reference)
Includes index and glossary.
Summary: Maps of each state in the United States, organized by region, accompanied by
facts and figures.
ISBN 0-439-47436-1
1. United States—Maps for children. 2. Children's atlases.   99-26960
[1. United States—Maps. 2. Atlases.] I. Title. II. Series.   CIP
G1200.R8 2000 <G&M>   MAPS
912.73—DC21

10 9 8 7 6 5 4 3 2 1   03 04 05/06 07

Printed in the U.S.A.   24

Reinforced Library Edition
ISBN: 0-439-55494-2
This edition, November 2003

Contents

How to Use This Book 6

New England	8
Connecticut	10
Maine	12
Massachusetts	14
New Hampshire	16
Rhode Island	18
Vermont	20

Mid-Atlantic	22
Delaware	24
Maryland	26
New Jersey	28
New York	30
Pennsylvania	32
Washington, D.C.	34

South	36
Alabama	38
Arkansas	40
Florida	42
Georgia	44
Kentucky	46
Louisiana	48
Mississippi	50
North Carolina	52
South Carolina	54
Tennessee	56
Virginia	58
West Virginia	60

Midwest	62
Illinois	64
Indiana	66
Iowa	68
Michigan	70
Minnesota	72
Missouri	74
Ohio	76
Wisconsin	78

Great Plains	80
Kansas	82
Nebraska	84
North Dakota	86
South Dakota	88

Mountain	90
Colorado	92
Idaho	94
Montana	96
Utah	98
Wyoming	100

Southwest	102
Arizona	104
Nevada	106
New Mexico	108
Oklahoma	110
Texas	112

Pacific	114
Alaska	116
California	118
Hawaii	120
Oregon	122
Washington	124

Appendices	126
Atlantic Possessions	128
Pacific Possessions	130
U.S. Population Density	132
Major U.S. River Systems	133
U.S. Geographic Regions	134
U.S. Territorial Expansion	135

Glossary 136
Index 138
Photo Credits 144

LEGEND
The legend printed above each map explains the meaning of its symbols, colors, and patterns. The legend also contains a scale, which shows the relationship of map distances to actual distances.

STATE NAME ORIGIN
Above the name of each state is an explanation of that name's origin.

STATE FLAG
Below the name of each state is a picture of that state's flag.

STATE LOCATOR MAP
This map shows the location of each state in relation to other continental states.

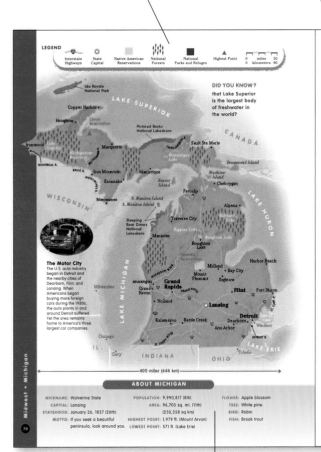

LEGEND

Interstate Highways	State Capital	Native American Reservations	National Forests	National Parks and Refuges	Highest Point	0 miles 50	
						0 kilometers 80	

Isle Royale National Park

LAKE SUPERIOR

Copper Harbor

Houghton

CANADA

DID YOU KNOW?
that Lake Superior is the largest body of freshwater in the world?

Ironwood

Pictured Rocks National Lakeshore

Marquette

Sault Ste. Marie

Drummond Island

Iron Mountain

Manistique

Mackinac Island

WISCONSIN

Escanaba

Benner Island

Petosky

Cheboygan

Menominee

N. Manitou Island
S. Manitou Island

Alpena

LAKE HURON

Traverse City

Sleeping Bear Dunes National Lakeshore

Higgins Lake

Manistee

Houghton Lake

Harbor Beach

The Motor City
The U.S. auto industry began in Detroit and the nearby cities of Dearborn, Flint, and Lansing. When Americans began buying more foreign cars during the 1980s, the auto plants in and around Detroit suffered. Yet the area remains home to America's three largest car companies.

Midland
Mount Pleasant
Bay City
Saginaw

Muskegon
Grand Rapids
Grand Haven
Flint
Port Huron

LAKE MICHIGAN

Milwaukee

Holland

Lansing

Detroit
Dearborn
Windsor

Kalamazoo
Battle Creek
Ann Arbor

Chicago

Gary

INDIANA

OHIO

Toledo

LAKE ERIE

←—— 400 miles (644 km) ——→

ABOUT MICHIGAN

NICKNAME: Wolverine State
CAPITAL: Lansing
STATEHOOD: January 26, 1837 (26th)
MOTTO: If you seek a beautiful peninsula, look around you.

POPULATION: 9,990,817 (8th)
AREA: 96,705 sq. mi. (11th) (250,358 sq km)
HIGHEST POINT: 1,979 ft. (Mount Arvon)
LOWEST POINT: 571 ft. (Lake Erie)

FLOWER: Apple blossom
TREE: White pine
BIRD: Robin
FISH: Brook trout

Midwest • Michigan

70

Michigan

A peninsula is a spit of land, shaped like a tongue, bounded on three sides by water. The state of Michigan is actually a pair of peninsulas, one divided from the other by the Straits of Mackinac (pronounced MACK-i-naw). Michigan's sometimes hilly, sometimes swampy Upper Peninsula is connected to the flatter, mitten-shaped Lower Peninsula by the Mackinac Bridge.

Michigan is called the Great Lakes State because it borders four of the five Great Lakes. As a result, shipping has always been an important business there. The locks at Sault Ste. Marie (nicknamed "the Soo") were opened in 1855 to service ships carrying timber and iron ore from Minnesota and the Upper Peninsula. These locks, which equalize the water level between Lake Superior and Lake Huron, are still among the world's busiest.

Michiganders in great numbers also use the Great Lakes for recreation. The rural Upper Peninsula doesn't have many people, but most of them fish. So do the carloads of Detroiters and Chicagoans who visit the Upper Peninsula each summer for a vacation out-of-doors. Despite the fact that it contains every one of Michigan's major cities and important industrial centers, the Lower Peninsula is no less outdoorsy. In fact, Michiganders of both peninsulas own more boats than residents of any other state.

The fish boil has been a Great Lakes tradition since the nineteenth century. It was devised by Scandinavian immigrants who wanted an easy way to cook whitefish and lake trout. For a traditional outdoor fish boil, Michiganders cook chunks of fish, potatoes, and onions in seasoned water over large wood fires.

75%

Michigan's Slice of the Pie
Michigan produces about 75 percent of the sour pie cherries grown in the United States. The area around Traverse City is particularly good for growing cherries because Lake Michigan moderates the weather there, tempering the frosts and cooling the orchards during summer.

Large ships haul cargo from the Midwest to the East (and beyond) using the St. Lawrence Seaway. This system of canals, locks, and dams joins the Great Lakes to the Atlantic Ocean.

71

STATE FACTS
This box lists useful information about each state. The numbers in parentheses refer to that state's rank among the fifty states. *Statehood* refers to the date that a state joined the Union. The population figures, provided by the Bureau of the Census, are estimates as of July 1, 2001 (the most recent estimates can be found online at www.census.gov).

Key to Metric Abbreviations
cm	centimeters
ha	hectares
kg	kilograms
km	kilometers
l	liters
m	meters
sq km	square kilometers

How to Use This Book

There are certain questions that an atlas can answer easily. For example: What's the capital of Kansas? Or: Which interstate highway runs between San Francisco and Los Angeles? The type of maps used in the *Scholastic Atlas of the United States* present this sort of information well. However, people often ask questions about the United States that maps can't answer. For instance: How are North Carolinians different from South Carolinians? Or: What makes Minnesotans special?

To answer these much more difficult questions, people usually turn to novelists, playwrights, and humorists, rather than mapmakers. Even so, there are facts about each state—who lives in it, what the people do, what the land is like—that can help students understand more about the quality of life there. You'll find many of these facts in the pages that follow, some presented in words and others in pictures. Perhaps not all your questions will be answered, but the description of each state provided will give you a good start.

One final note: The statistics presented in this book are the most recent that were available when the book was updated in 2002. Most reflect data from 2000 and 2001.

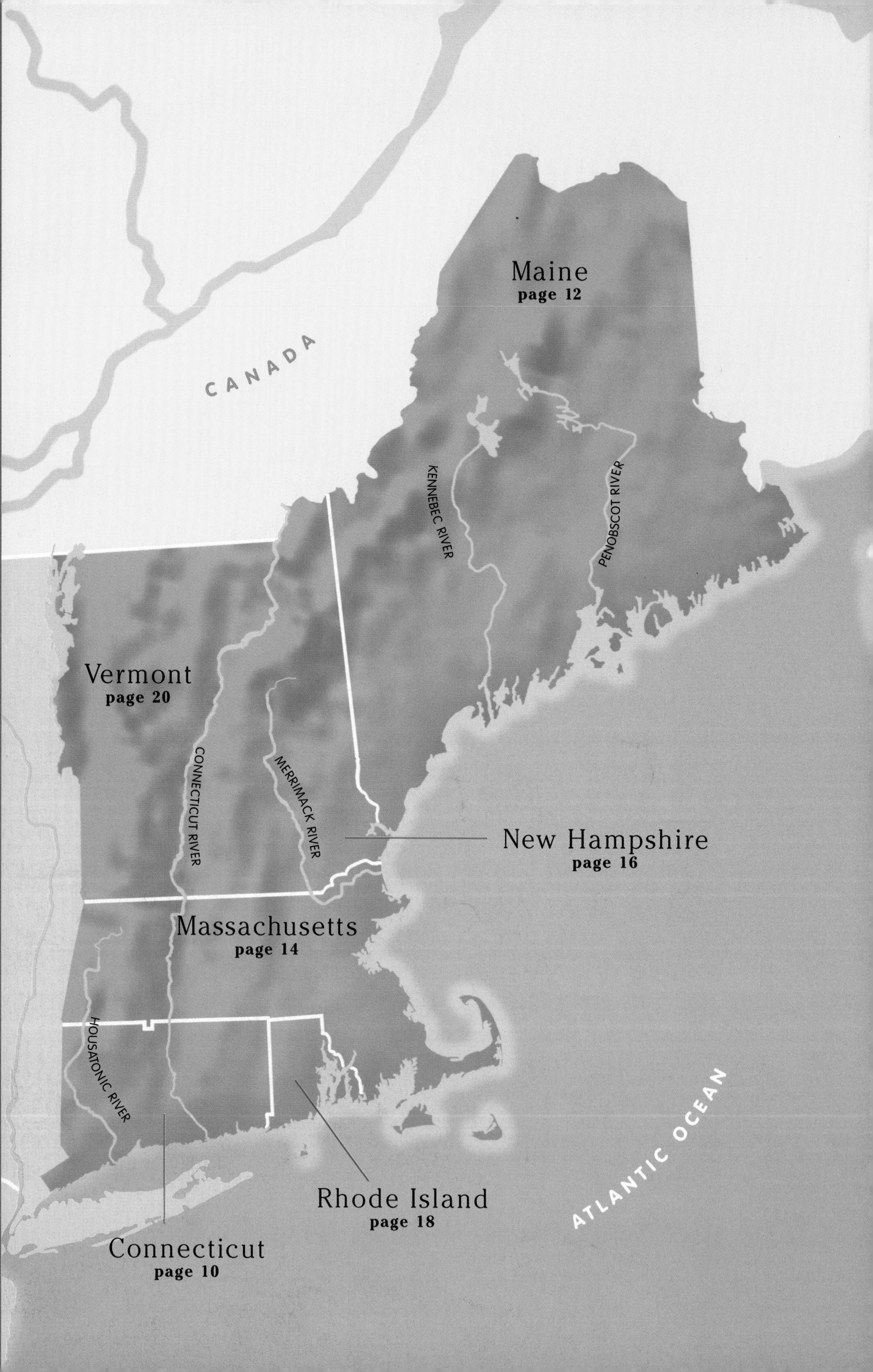

Maine
page 12

CANADA

KENNEBEC RIVER

PENOBSCOT RIVER

Vermont
page 20

CONNECTICUT RIVER

MERRIMACK RIVER

New Hampshire
page 16

Massachusetts
page 14

HOUSATONIC RIVER

Rhode Island
page 18

ATLANTIC OCEAN

Connecticut
page 10

New England

The Appalachian Mountain chain, which runs from Alabama all the way north to Canada, dominates the topography of New England. Among other ranges, the Appalachians include the Green Mountains of Vermont, the White Mountains of New Hampshire, and the Longfellow Mountains of Maine. The region's most important waterway is the Connecticut River, whose valley separates the Western New England Uplands from the slightly less hilly Eastern New England Uplands.

🛣 20 — Interstate Highways
★ — State Capital
▲ — Highest Point

miles 0 — 25
kilometers 0 — 40

The Insurance City

The U.S. insurance industry, which began in Connecticut, has been headquartered in Hartford for more than two hundred years. During the eighteenth century, Hartford firms insured ships and cargoes. Later, they pioneered other types of coverage, such as accident and automobile insurance.

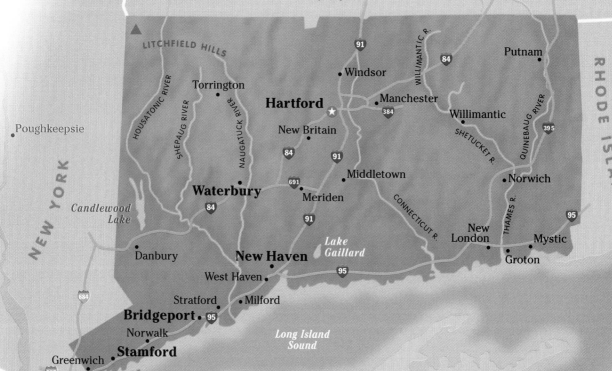

MASSACHUSETTS

Springfield

LITCHFIELD HILLS

91 Windsor

84 Putnam

HOUSATONIC RIVER
SHEPAUG RIVER
NAUGATUCK RIVER

Torrington

Hartford ★ Manchester
384
WILLIMANTIC R.

Poughkeepsie

New Britain
84
91
Willimantic
SHETUCKET R.
QUINEBAUG RIVER
395

NEW YORK

691 Middletown
Waterbury
84 Meriden
Norwich
THAMES R.
95

Candlewood Lake

91
Lake Gaillard
CONNECTICUT R.
New London
Mystic

Danbury **New Haven**
West Haven
95
Groton

684
Stratford Milford

Bridgeport 95
Norwalk
Long Island Sound
Stamford
Greenwich
287

New York City

RHODE ISLAND

ATLANTIC OCEAN

DID YOU KNOW?

that Hartford resident Mark Twain once said of the state's changeable climate, "If you don't like Connecticut weather, wait a minute"?

◄———— 90 miles (145 km) ————►

ABOUT CONNECTICUT

NICKNAME: Constitution State
CAPITAL: Hartford
STATEHOOD: January 9, 1788 (5th)
MOTTO: He who transplanted sustains.

POPULATION: 3,425,074 (29th)
AREA: 5,544 sq. mi. (48th)
(14,353 sq km)
HIGHEST POINT: 2,380 ft. (Mount Frissell)
LOWEST POINT: Sea level (Long Island Sound)

FLOWER: Mountain laurel
TREE: White oak
BIRD: American robin

Connecticut

Today, most people think of Yankees as baseball players. However, when novelist Mark Twain wrote *A Connecticut Yankee in King Arthur's Court* in 1889, he used the word *Yankee* to mean "someone from New England."

Connecticut Yankees were, for Twain, a special breed: They were tinkerers with a knack for making things. Because Connecticut can claim no oil or mineral wealth, residents have had to rely on "Yankee ingenuity" for their prosperity. Products invented in Connecticut include the revolver (by Samuel Colt in 1835), vulcanized rubber (by Charles Goodyear in 1839), and the cylinder lock (by Linus Yale in 1861). Even today, manufacturing is a crucial part of the state's economic success, especially the production of military transport equipment. Factories in Bridgeport turn out helicopters (invented in Connecticut in 1939), while highly skilled workers assemble jet engines in East Hartford and nuclear submarines in Groton.

Although the Connecticut River Valley is quite fertile, the thin, rocky soil on either side of it makes farming elsewhere in Connecticut difficult. To the west of the river, the land rises into the Litchfield Hills, where the state's highest elevations are found. On the other side of the Connecticut River, the land slopes down to the southeast. Along the state's southern border are marshy coastal lowlands that drain into Long Island Sound. This coastal plain and the Connecticut River Valley, both relatively flat, hold most of Connecticut's larger cities.

Native American Gaming
Although gambling is generally illegal in Connecticut, the state contains two of the world's largest casinos: the Mohegan Sun and Foxwoods, both near New London. These casinos are allowed to operate because they belong to Native American groups, which are treated legally as independent nations existing within the United States.

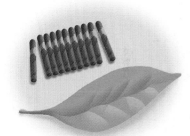

Wrap It Up
What little agriculture Connecticut does have involves mostly direct-to-market products, such as flowering plants, fresh vegetables, and Christmas trees. The one important exception is shade-grown tobacco leaf. The best Connecticut River Valley leaves, about twenty-four inches (61 cm) long, are used to wrap cigars.

Judging by per-capita income, Connecticut is the nation's richest state. Its wealthiest area, Fairfield County, nearly borders New York City. Residents there include many well-paid corporate executives who commute to jobs in Manhattan.

🛣 20 Interstate Highways

⭐ State Capital

⬛ National Parks and Refuges

🌲 National Forests

🔺 Highest Point

0 miles 50
0 kilometers 80

Parlez Vous?

There are no minorities to speak of in Maine, which is 98 percent white. However, many of those whites are transplanted French Canadians for whom English is a second language. Much of Maine is bilingual, and in the St. John River Valley, French is the dominant tongue.

DID YOU KNOW?

that the 2,034-mile-long (3,273-kilometer-long) Appalachian Trail ends at Mount Katahdin, Maine's highest point? Because of its height, Mount Katahdin is also the first place that the sun strikes the continental United States.

207 miles (333 km)

ABOUT MAINE

NICKNAME: Pine Tree State	**POPULATION:** 1,286,670 (40th)	**FLOWER:** White pinecone and tassel
CAPITAL: Augusta	**AREA:** 35,387 sq. mi. (39th)	**TREE:** White pine
STATEHOOD: March 15, 1820 (23rd)	(91,613 sq km)	**BIRD:** Chickadee
MOTTO: I direct.	**HIGHEST POINT:** 5,267 ft. (Mount Katahdin)	**FISH:** Landlocked salmon
	LOWEST POINT: Sea level (Atlantic Ocean)	

Maine

Maine is large, with about as much land as the rest of New England combined. It's also roomy, with a population only slightly larger than that of Rhode Island. In fact, Maine is the least densely populated state east of the Mississippi River. This is especially true north of Bangor, where the terrain becomes mountainous, heavily forested, and sometimes impassable.

That's why most Mainers live in towns along one of the state's tidal rivers or in fishing villages along the Atlantic coast. In the north, many Mainers earn their livings from the timber industry, while in the south, tourism pays a large share of the bills. The southern coast from Kittery to Casco Bay is particularly popular with vacationers, who rent houses during the summer to enjoy Maine's scenic beauty and cool temperatures. (The ocean water is usually too cold for swimming.)

Beyond their skill at trapping lobsters, native Mainers are also celebrated for their industriousness and endurance. Their state's environment is harsh, with long bitter winters and a challenging landscape. Yet, since the first English settlers landed in 1607, the people of Maine have shown remarkable perseverance in response to these environmental challenges. As a result, they have achieved a national cultural importance far beyond their economic and political status.

Maine's generally poor soil supports very little agriculture. That's not the case in Aroostook County, however, where potato farms compete with those in Idaho. Income from potatoes is so important to northeastern Maine that schools regularly excuse students so they can help out with the fall harvest.

Maine's Annual Lobster Catch

	$180 Million
	$150 Million
	$120 Million
	$90 Million
1995 1996 1997 1998 1999 2000	

Fishing has long been an important part of the Maine economy, and lobsters, which flourish in the state's cool coastal waters, remain the most valuable catch. However, rising prices have encouraged overfishing, and ecologists now worry that the future of the Maine lobster could be threatened.

During the last Ice Age, glaciers carved Maine's rocky shoreline into scenic cliffs, bays, coves, and beaches. Maine's numerous offshore islands are mostly the tops of hills submerged when those glaciers melted and the sea level rose.

LEGEND

 Interstate Highways

 State Capital

■ National Parks and Refuges

Marshlands

▲ Highest Point

| 0 | miles | 25 |
| 0 | kilometers | 40 |

DID YOU KNOW?

that there's a Lake Chargoggagoggmanchauggauggag-
oggchaubunagungamaugg near Worcester? This Native
American name means "You fish on your side; I fish on
my side; nobody fishes in the middle."

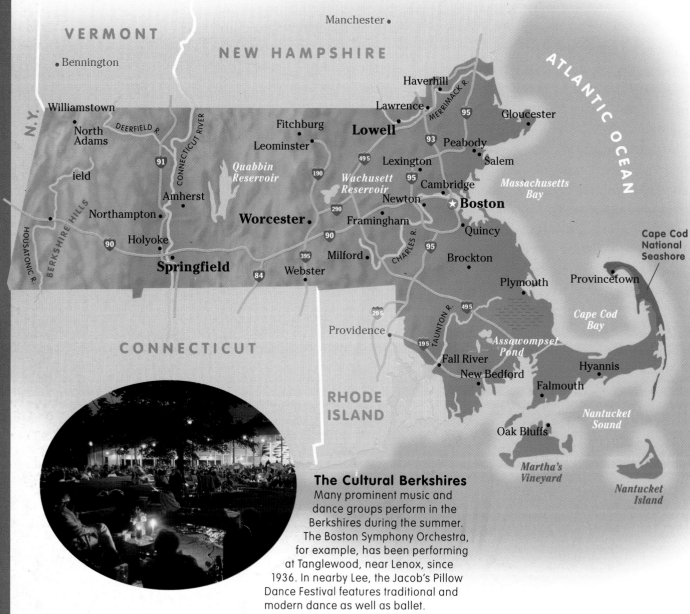

VERMONT

NEW HAMPSHIRE

Manchester

Bennington

N.Y.

Williamstown

North Adams

...ield

DEERFIELD R.

91

CONNECTICUT RIVER

Quabbin Reservoir

Amherst

Northampton

BERKSHIRE HILLS

HOUSATONIC R.

90 Holyoke

Springfield

84 Webster

395 Milford

Worcester

290 Framingham

190 Wachusett Reservoir

Fitchburg

Leominster

Lexington

495

95

Newton

Cambridge

★ Boston

Quincy

CHARLES R.

95 Brockton

Haverhill

Lawrence

MERRIMACK R.

95

93 Peabody

Salem

Gloucester

Lowell

Massachusetts Bay

ATLANTIC OCEAN

Cape Cod National Seashore

Provincetown

Plymouth

295

Providence

TAUNTON R.

195

Fall River

New Bedford

495

Assawompset Pond

Cape Cod Bay

Hyannis

Falmouth

Nantucket Sound

Oak Bluffs

Martha's Vineyard

Nantucket Island

CONNECTICUT

RHODE ISLAND

The Cultural Berkshires
Many prominent music and
dance groups perform in the
Berkshires during the summer.
The Boston Symphony Orchestra,
for example, has been performing
at Tanglewood, near Lenox, since
1936. In nearby Lee, the Jacob's Pillow
Dance Festival features traditional and
modern dance as well as ballet.

◄———— 190 miles (306 km) ————►

ABOUT MASSACHUSETTS

NICKNAME: Bay State

CAPITAL: Boston

STATEHOOD: February 6, 1788 (6th)

MOTTO: By the sword we seek
peace, but peace only
under liberty.

POPULATION: 6,379,304 (13th)

AREA: 10,555 sq. mi. (44th)
(27,326 sq km)

HIGHEST POINT: 3,487 ft. (Mount Greylock)

LOWEST POINT: Sea level (Atlantic Ocean)

FLOWER: Mayflower

TREE: American elm

BIRD: Chickadee

FISH: Cod

Massachusetts

When people talk about the United States as a "melting pot" of many different cultures, Massachusetts provides a ready example. Although Yankee Protestants dominated the colony for two hundred years, the textile mills that opened near Boston during the nineteenth century attracted a flood of immigrants. First came the Irish, then the French Canadians, then the Italians and other Europeans. The textile mills are gone now, but Massachusetts remains a top manufacturing state, with a population that's still ethnically diverse.

New Bedford, for example, contains the largest community of Portuguese Americans. The great-great-grandfathers of these people came to America to work in the whaling industry. Now many of their descendants work as commercial fishermen and in fish-processing plants. On the other hand, Boston is predominantly Irish, famous for its long string of Irish mayors. Of course, it's also the financial capital of New England, as well as the region's population center. Massachusetts has nearly as many residents as the other five New England states combined, and half of these people live in the Boston area.

Along with the rest of the Massachusetts coastline, Boston sits on the sandy Atlantic Coastal Plain. Inland, the land rises slowly into the rocky New England Uplands. The fertile Connecticut River Valley, which divides the state, separates the southern fringe of the White Mountains (in the east) from the Berkshire Hills (in the west).

Silicon Valley East
Among the most successful businesses in Massachusetts are the technology firms lining Route 128 west of Boston. These companies have taken particular advantage of the high-tech workforce being created by such local (yet nationally prominent) universities as Harvard and the Massachusetts Institute of Technology.

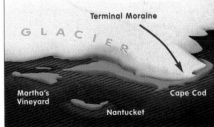

End of the Line
Cape Cod, a sandy peninsula sixty-five miles (105 km) long, is what geologists call a terminal moraine. It marks the farthest point reached by the glacier that carved out the Connecticut River Valley. It's also the line along which the melting glacier deposited all the rocky debris it had been carrying.

Cranberries grow in bogs, or areas of wet spongy ground, that are usually flooded at harvesttime. Although the state's generally poor soil supports little agriculture, the cranberry bogs of southeastern Massachusetts produce nearly 40 percent of the nation's crop.

LEGEND

🛡20	⊛	■	🌲	▲	0 ——— miles ——— 25
Interstate Highways	State Capital	National Parks and Refuges	National Forests	Highest Point	0 ——— miles ——— 40

Although most people think of New Hampshire as primarily rural, it contains significant manufacturing. The most heavily industrialized area is Manchester, New Hampshire's largest city, where factories make machinery, computers, military communications equipment, and plastics.

DID YOU KNOW?

that New Hampshire's state representatives, who are paid just one hundred dollars a year, haven't gotten a raise since 1784?

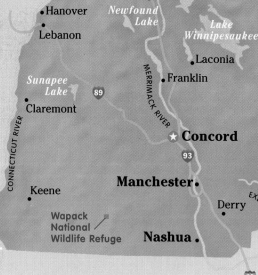

CANADA

HALLS STREAM

Connecticut Lakes

ANDROSCOGGIN R.

Umbagog Lake

• Berlin

St. Johnsbury

• Littleton

MAINE

▲ WHITE MOUNTAINS

🛡93

VERMONT

Conway

Plymouth

Squam Lake

• Hanover

Newfound Lake

Lake Winnipesaukee

Portland •

Great East Lake

• Lebanon

• Laconia

SALMON FALLS RIVER

Sunapee Lake

🛡89

• Franklin

• Rochester

• Claremont

MERRIMACK RIVER

CONNECTICUT RIVER

☆ **Concord**

Dover •

PISCATAQUA RIVER

🛡93

Portsmouth •

ATLANTIC OCEAN

Manchester •

Exeter •

🛡95

• Keene

Derry •

EXETER RIVER

Brattleboro •

Wapack National Wildlife Refuge

Nashua •

MASSACHUSETTS

🛡93

• Lowell

◄———— 93 miles (150 km) ————►

ABOUT NEW HAMPSHIRE

NICKNAME: Granite State

CAPITAL: Concord

STATEHOOD: June 21, 1788 (9th)

MOTTO: Live free or die.

POPULATION: 1,259,181 (41st)

AREA: 9,351 sq. mi. (46th) (24,209 sq km)

HIGHEST POINT: 6,288 ft. (Mount Washington)

LOWEST POINT: Sea level (Atlantic Ocean)

FLOWER: Purple lilac

TREE: White birch

BIRD: Purple finch

FISH: Brook trout, striped bass

New Hampshire

More than most Americans, the residents of New Hampshire honor the country's past and attempt to preserve older visions of the way people's lives should be run. Citizens of other states typically have little contact with their local governments, yet towns in New Hampshire still hold open meetings to decide important public issues. In general, the people of New Hampshire believe strongly in exercising their political voices, and this is particularly true every four years when the state hosts its traditional "first in the nation" presidential primary.

In northern New Hampshire, where the stony White Mountains dominate the landscape, most people live in small towns that depend on lumber for their livelihood. Like Connecticut, it's a place of enduring Yankee values, where the highly conservative residents (nearly all of whom are white) are often compared to the granite bedrock underlying the state. The only industrial center is Berlin, where large mills process trees into paper and wood pulp.

South of the White Mountains, however, New Hampshire contains a number of large urban centers that house about 85 percent of the state's population. People originally concentrated in these cities because southern New Hampshire is highly industrialized. Lately, however, more and more people have been moving from Boston to suburban New Hampshire to escape the city and Massachusetts state taxes. New Hampshire has neither an income tax nor a sales tax.

Every year on the first Tuesday in March, citizens of New Hampshire take part in a tradition dating back to colonial times: the town meeting. Before the spring thaw comes and mud makes some roads impassable, town residents gather to vote on school budgets, property taxes, and other government matters.

Top Wind Speed: 231 miles per hour (372 km/hr)

The Windiest Place on Earth
Atop Mount Washington, the highest peak in New England, the National Weather Service operates a climate research station. On April 12, 1934, this station's instruments registered a world-record wind speed of 231 miles per hour. Normally, winter gusts on Mount Washington range from 120 to 160 miles (193 to 257 km) per hour.

In a Native American language once spoken in New Hampshire, *monadnock* means "mountain that stands alone." More recently, Mount Monadnock near Keene has given its name to isolated plugs of granite that become mountains once the surrounding land has eroded away.

17

LEGEND

🛣 20	✪	▨	▨	▨	▲	0 miles 10
Interstate Highways	State Capital	Native American Reservations	National Parks and Refuges	Marshlands	Highest Point	0 kilometers 16

During the late nineteenth century, Newport was perhaps the world's most fashionable resort. The richest Americans built summer "cottages" there along the famous Newport Cliff Walk. The grandest of these mansions is the seventy-room Breakers, built by the Vanderbilt family in 1892.

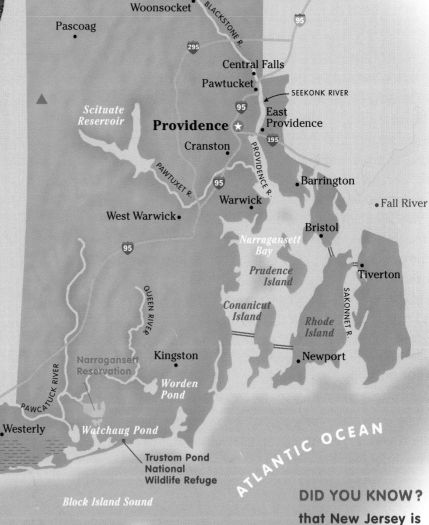

MASSACHUSETTS

Woonsocket

Pascoag

BLACKSTONE R.

295

95

Central Falls

Pawtucket

SEEKONK RIVER

Scituate Reservoir

95

East Providence

Providence ✪

Cranston

PROVIDENCE R.

195

PAWTUXET R.

95

Barrington

Warwick

Fall River

West Warwick

Bristol

95

Narragansett Bay

Prudence Island

Tiverton

SAKONNET R.

CONNECTICUT

QUEEN RIVER

Conanicut Island

Rhode Island

Narragansett Reservation

Kingston

Newport

PAWCATUCK RIVER

Worden Pond

PAWCATUCK RIVER

Westerly

Watchaug Pond

Trustom Pond National Wildlife Refuge

ATLANTIC OCEAN

Block Island Sound

Block Island

DID YOU KNOW?

that New Jersey is the only state more densely populated than Rhode Island?

◄------------------- 37 miles (60 km) -------------------►

ABOUT RHODE ISLAND

NICKNAME: Ocean State

CAPITAL: Providence

STATEHOOD: May 29, 1790 (13th)

MOTTO: Hope.

POPULATION: 1,058,920 (43rd)

AREA: 1,545 sq. mi. (50th)
(4,000 sq km)

HIGHEST POINT: 812 ft. (Jerimoth Hill)

LOWEST POINT: Sea level (Atlantic Ocean)

FLOWER: Violet

TREE: Red maple

BIRD: Rhode Island red (chicken)

Rhode Island

Because Rhode Island is the smallest state, it's particularly easy for Rhode Islanders to travel—that is, they don't have to go very far to reach Massachusetts or Connecticut. Yet people there will tell you that Rhode Islanders like to stay close to home. Part of the reason is that they're proud of where they live, even though there's so little of it.

Since the founding of the colony by Protestant dissidents in 1636, Rhode Islanders have championed religious tolerance. Those who have benefited include Jews, who in 1763 established the first synagogue in the colonies in Newport, and Roman Catholics, who immigrated to the state in large numbers once Rhode Island began to industrialize during the nineteenth century.

The state had little choice but to industrialize. Because of its poor soil, agriculture wasn't an option. So, relying on their reputation for fine craftsmanship, Rhode Islanders built factories instead. These factories, in turn, attracted workers from other countries who diversified the mostly white, mostly Protestant population. Today, Rhode Island has a higher percentage of Roman Catholics than any other state, with large Irish and Italian communities in Providence and French Canadians in Woonsocket.

The island for which the state is named is the largest of thirty-five in Narragansett Bay, where sand beaches and salt marshes dominate the terrain. On the mainland, however, the lowlands of the Atlantic Coastal Plain quickly give way to the low, rocky hills of the New England Uplands.

Factories in Providence began making costume jewelry in 1794, and the city remains a national leader in the field. Designed to be trendy and disposable, these fashion accessories are affordable because they're made from inexpensive materials rather than precious metals and gemstones.

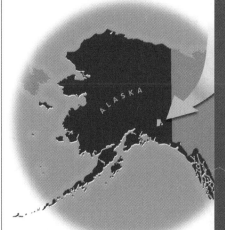

A Tiny Fraction of the Size
Rhode Island is so small that it would take 425 Rhode Islands to fill up just one Alaska, the largest of the fifty states.

Although freighters use it to reach the busy port of Providence, Narragansett Bay is best known for its water sports. In particular, it's the focus of yachting on the Atlantic coast.

LEGEND

Interstate Highways	State Capital	National Forests	Highest Point	0 miles 25	0 kilometers 40

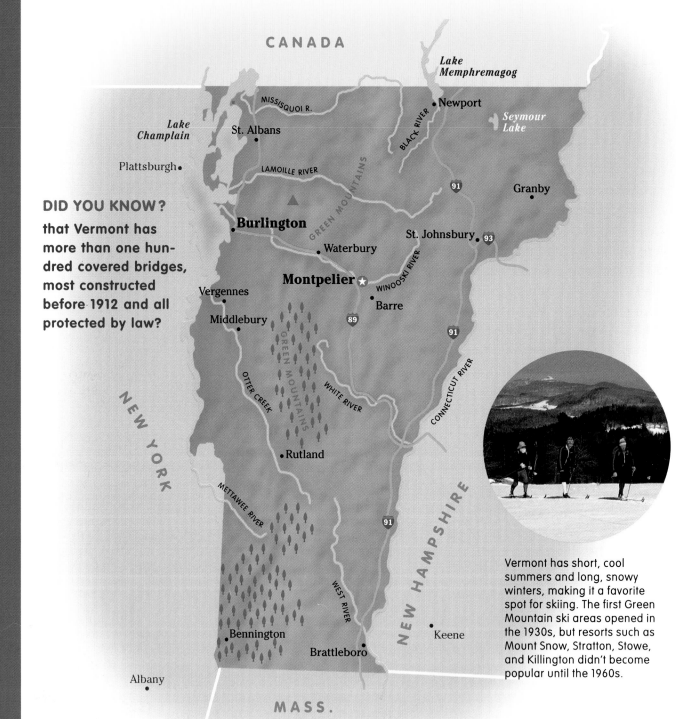

CANADA

Lake Memphremagog

MISSISQUOI R.

Lake Champlain

St. Albans

Newport

Seymour Lake

BLACK RIVER

Plattsburgh

LAMOILLE RIVER

91

Granby

DID YOU KNOW?

that Vermont has more than one hundred covered bridges, most constructed before 1912 and all protected by law?

GREEN MOUNTAINS

Burlington

Waterbury

St. Johnsbury

93

Montpelier

WINOOSKI RIVER

Vergennes

Barre

Middlebury

89

91

OTTER CREEK

GREEN MOUNTAINS

WHITE RIVER

CONNECTICUT RIVER

NEW YORK

METTAWEE RIVER

Rutland

NEW HAMPSHIRE

91

WEST RIVER

Bennington

Keene

Brattleboro

Albany

Vermont has short, cool summers and long, snowy winters, making it a favorite spot for skiing. The first Green Mountain ski areas opened in the 1930s, but resorts such as Mount Snow, Stratton, Stowe, and Killington didn't become popular until the 1960s.

MASS.

← 90 miles (145 km) →

ABOUT VERMONT

NICKNAME: Green Mountain State	**POPULATION:** 613,090 (49th)	**FLOWER:** Red clover
CAPITAL: Montpelier	**AREA:** 9,615 sq. mi. (45th)	**TREE:** Sugar maple
STATEHOOD: March 4, 1791 (14th)	(24,892 sq km)	**BIRD:** Hermit thrush
MOTTO: Freedom and unity.	**HIGHEST POINT:** 4,393 ft. (Mount Mansfield)	**FISH:** Brook trout, walleye pike
	LOWEST POINT: 95 ft. (Lake Champlain)	

Vermont

Vermont is a small-town state. Montpelier, the smallest state capital, contains just eight thousand residents, and Vermont's other cities aren't much larger. In fact, about as many people live in Boston as live in all of Vermont. Even the factories there are small: Four out of five employ fewer than fifty people.

As late as the 1950s, the typical Vermonter was a Protestant of English descent, and the state is still 99 percent white. Following the social upheaval of the 1960s, however, many young people moved to Vermont, hoping for a simpler, more natural lifestyle. One result of this influx (and the new sensibility brought by these people) has been the development of a new economically important specialty foods market in the state. Products such as goat cheese, organic vegetables, and emu burgers now proudly bear the "Made in Vermont" label and sell nationwide.

Like its neighbors, Vermont is mountainous; yet unlike the other New England states, Vermont depends heavily on agriculture. Crops aren't very profitable, because only the Connecticut River Valley has suitable soil, so most Vermont farmers raise livestock instead. Dairy cows happily graze on most mountainsides, producing the milk used to make Vermont's famous cheddar cheese.

The heavily forested Green Mountains that give Vermont its name are the backbone of the state, running north to south in a band about thirty miles (50 km) wide. The rest of the state is mostly hill country cut by fast-flowing streams.

Milk accounts for about two thirds of Vermont's farm income. Traditionally, that milk has gone to make cheddar cheese. However, some of it now goes to the Ben & Jerry's ice cream factory in Waterbury. With flavors such as Rainforest Crunch and Cherry Garcia, founders Ben Cohen and Jerry Greenfield have used 1960s sensibilities to promote their product.

Vermont leads the nation in maple syrup production, which the locals call sugaring. Maple sap begins to flow in early spring, when daytime temperatures first rise above 40°F (5°C) yet nighttime temperatures remain below freezing. Sugarmakers boil down the sap from four trees, about forty gallons (150 l), to make a single gallon (3.8 l) of syrup.

Poet Robert Frost once described fall in the Green Mountains as a time when the "leaves go to glory." About three out of every four Vermonters live either on farms or in small towns like this one.

CANADA

New York
page 30

LAKE ONTARIO

MOHAWK RIVER

ERIE CANAL

LAKE ERIE

ALLEGHENY RIVER

HUDSON RIVER

OHIO RIVER

Pennsylvania
page 32

SUSQUEHANNA RIVER

DELAWARE RIVER

New
Jersey
page 28

MONONGAHELA RIVER

Maryland
page 26

POTOMAC RIVER

Delaware
page 24

Washington,
D.C.
page 34

ATLANTIC OCEAN

Every Mid-Atlantic state sits—at least in some small part—on both the Piedmont Plateau and the Atlantic Coastal Plain. The line along which these two regions meet is called the fall line because the land there drops sharply. Two hundred years ago, George Washington chose the point at which the fall line crosses the Potomac River for the location of his new federal city. Hikers today can easily tell when they're near the fall line because of all the rapids and waterfalls it creates.

Mid-Atlantic

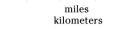

Interstate Highways	State Capital	National Parks and Refuges	Marshlands	Highest Point	0 miles 25 0 kilometers 40	

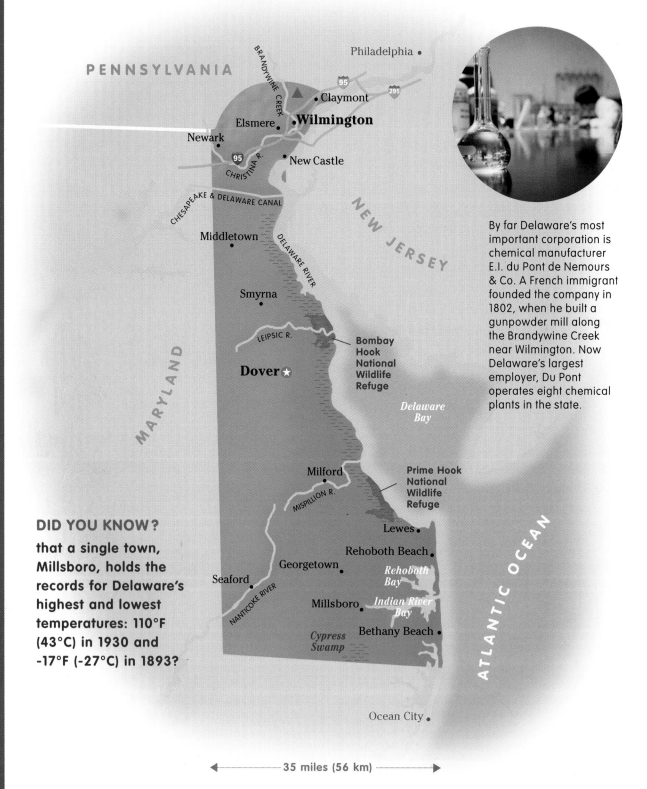

PENNSYLVANIA

Philadelphia

Claymont

Wilmington

Elsmere

Newark

New Castle

CHRISTINA R.

BRANDYWINE CREEK

NEW JERSEY

CHESAPEAKE & DELAWARE CANAL

Middletown

DELAWARE RIVER

Smyrna

LEIPSIC R.

Bombay Hook National Wildlife Refuge

Dover

Delaware Bay

MARYLAND

Milford

Prime Hook National Wildlife Refuge

MISPILLION R.

Lewes

Rehoboth Beach

Georgetown

Rehoboth Bay

Seaford

Millsboro

Indian River Bay

NANTICOKE RIVER

Bethany Beach

Cypress Swamp

ATLANTIC OCEAN

Ocean City

35 miles (56 km)

By far Delaware's most important corporation is chemical manufacturer E.I. du Pont de Nemours & Co. A French immigrant founded the company in 1802, when he built a gunpowder mill along the Brandywine Creek near Wilmington. Now Delaware's largest employer, Du Pont operates eight chemical plants in the state.

DID YOU KNOW?

that a single town, Millsboro, holds the records for Delaware's highest and lowest temperatures: 110°F (43°C) in 1930 and -17°F (-27°C) in 1893?

ABOUT DELAWARE

NICKNAME: First State	**POPULATION:** 796,165 (45th)	**FLOWER:** Peach blossom
CAPITAL: Dover	**AREA:** 2,489 sq. mi. (49th)	**TREE:** American holly
STATEHOOD: December 7, 1787 (1st)	(6,444 sq km)	**BIRD:** Blue hen chicken
MOTTO: Liberty and independence.	**HIGHEST POINT:** 448 ft. (Ebright Road)	**FISH:** Weakfish
	LOWEST POINT: Sea level (Atlantic Ocean)	

Delaware

In Delaware, everyone seems to know everyone else. Of course that's not literally true, yet the state is small enough that its residents cross paths often. Because of this, Delaware is the sort of place where much business gets done in restaurants and at social gatherings.

After chemicals—that is, after Du Pont—Delaware's biggest business is incorporation. Of the five hundred largest U.S. companies, more than half are Delaware corporations. This may seem odd for such a small state, but Delaware has been passing laws to attract corporations since 1899. Although nearly all of these companies do business elsewhere, they've incorporated in Delaware because of the state's low taxation, up-to-date laws, and experienced judges. In return, they provide work for armies of lawyers, accountants, and other business professionals familiar with the state's legal requirements and procedures. Overall, corporate taxes and fees make up more than one fifth of Delaware's total revenue.

Delaware sits on the Delmarva Peninsula, which separates the Chesapeake Bay from the Atlantic Ocean. The Chesapeake & Delaware Canal, linking these two bodies of water, provides an important boundary between the state's industrial north and its agricultural south. Northern Delaware contains about two thirds of the state's population and all of its major transportation routes, while the main industry in the south is chicken farming.

The Brandywine Valley north of Wilmington is called Chateau Country because of its many Du Pont family mansions. Two have become museums: Winterthur (pictured above) houses the nation's finest collection of early American decorative arts, while the Hagley Museum, on the site of the original Du Pont powder works, documents life during the nineteenth century.

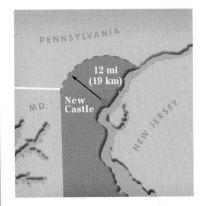

Delaware is the only state with a partially rounded border, the result of a land dispute during the early 1680s. At that time, William Penn and the Duke of York agreed that the boundary between Pennsylvania and Delaware would be an arc "drawn at twelve miles' distance from New Castle."

The salt marshes and estuaries that line Delaware Bay provide excellent habitats for birds and shellfish. Delaware's strict shoreline protection laws, the first of their kind in the nation, forbid pollution-causing factories too close to the bay.

LEGEND

🛣 20	⭐	⬛	〜〜〜	▲	
Interstate Highways	State Capital	National Parks and Refuges	Marshlands	Highest Point	0 miles 25 / 0 kilometers 40

DID YOU KNOW?

that a Baltimore law makes it illegal to take a lion to the movies?

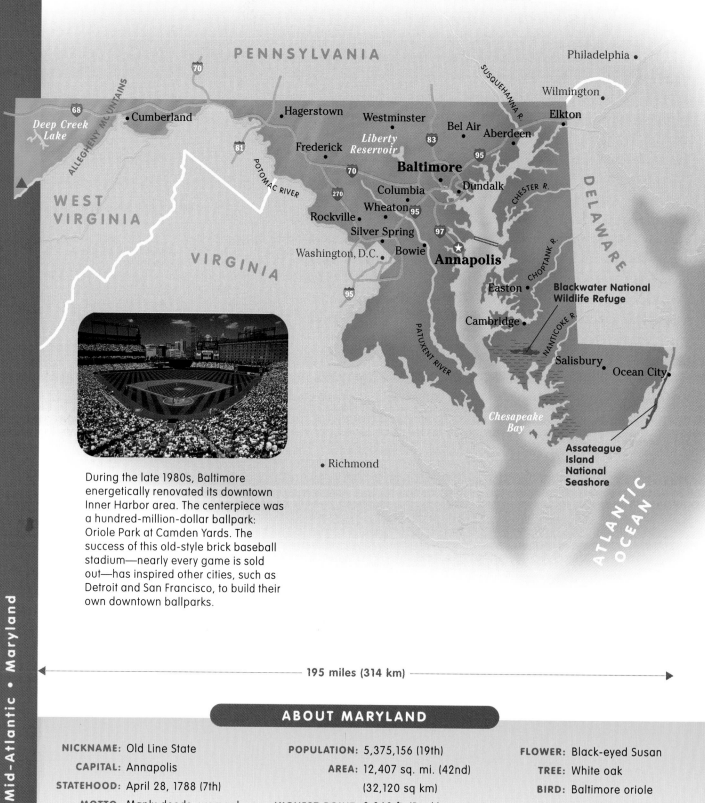

PENNSYLVANIA

Philadelphia •

SUSQUEHANNA R.

Wilmington •

• Cumberland

Deep Creek Lake

ALLEGHENY MOUNTAINS

• Hagerstown

Westminster •

Bel Air •

Aberdeen •

Elkton •

DELAWARE

WEST VIRGINIA

Frederick •

Liberty Reservoir

Baltimore

CHESTER R.

• Dundalk

POTOMAC RIVER

Columbia •

Wheaton •

Rockville •

Silver Spring •

Washington, D.C. •

Bowie •

Annapolis ⭐

CHOPTANK R.

VIRGINIA

Easton •

Blackwater National Wildlife Refuge

Cambridge •

NANTICOKE R.

PATUXENT RIVER

Salisbury •

Ocean City •

• Richmond

Chesapeake Bay

Assateague Island National Seashore

ATLANTIC OCEAN

During the late 1980s, Baltimore energetically renovated its downtown Inner Harbor area. The centerpiece was a hundred-million-dollar ballpark: Oriole Park at Camden Yards. The success of this old-style brick baseball stadium—nearly every game is sold out—has inspired other cities, such as Detroit and San Francisco, to build their own downtown ballparks.

195 miles (314 km)

ABOUT MARYLAND

NICKNAME: Old Line State

CAPITAL: Annapolis

STATEHOOD: April 28, 1788 (7th)

MOTTO: Manly deeds, womanly words.

POPULATION: 5,375,156 (19th)

AREA: 12,407 sq. mi. (42nd) (32,120 sq km)

HIGHEST POINT: 3,360 ft. (Backbone Mt.)

LOWEST POINT: Sea level (Atlantic Ocean)

FLOWER: Black-eyed Susan

TREE: White oak

BIRD: Baltimore oriole

FISH: Rockfish

Maryland

Maryland has so many different looks that what you see depends on what you're looking for. If you're looking for people, you'll find most of them living between Washington, D.C., and Baltimore. Three out of every four Marylanders live in this densely populated corridor because most of the jobs are there. The leading industries are electrical equipment and food processing, but the federal government is also a major employer. Many Marylanders commute to jobs in D.C., but even more work at federal facilities in Maryland.

If you're looking for land, you'll find that most of the state is rural. On Maryland's Eastern Shore, part of the Atlantic Coastal Plain, farmers raise broiler chickens inland while resort towns line the Atlantic beaches. In western Maryland, atop the hilly Piedmont, fertile farmland is occasionally interrupted by large belts of clay. (This clay provided the raw material for the bricks that have made Maryland's homes and factories so distinctive.) Farther west, in the section of the state called the "bird's wing" because of its odd shape, the land rises sharply into the Allegheny Mountains.

Finally, even if you're not looking for water, you'll find it impossible to miss Chesapeake Bay, the largest estuary in the United States. The bay was formed at the end of the last Ice Age when rising seawater flooded the southern Susquehanna River Valley. Today, the bay is 193 miles (311 km) long with 3,200 miles (5,200 km) of shoreline.

Maryland's older industrial look often appeals to feature-film makers in search of colorful urban locations. Among the first directors to shoot films in Baltimore were home-grown talents Barry Levinson (*Diner, Avalon*) and John Waters (*Hairspray, Cry-Baby*). The city now expects to host two or three major productions each year.

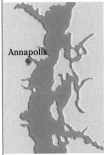
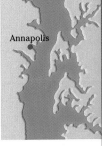

1795   1995

Shifting Shoreline
Maryland's shoreline has been frustrating mapmakers for centuries. The problem is that the tidal waters of Chesapeake Bay keep rearranging the land, filling in swamps as they wash away islands.

Although pollution and overfishing have dramatically reduced the oyster and striped bass populations, Chesapeake Bay still produces about one hundred million pounds (45 million kg) of seafood each year, including fifty million pounds (23 million kg) of blue crab.

Interstate Highways

State Capital

National Parks and Refuges

Marshlands

Highest Point

| 0 | miles | 25 |
| 0 | kilometers | 40 |

New Jersey has one of the busiest and most extensive transportation systems in the world. The trucking, shipping, and air routes that converge at Newark make use of the New Jersey Turnpike (the busiest U.S. toll road), the Port of Newark, and Newark Airport.

NEW YORK

KITTATINNY MTS.

Greenwood Lake

Lake Hopatcong

Wanaque Reservoir

HUDSON RIVER

80

Paterson

Dover

Clifton

Hoboken

New York City

287

Newark

Jersey City

78

Elizabeth

Bayonne

DELAWARE RIVER

Plainfield

278

Edison

Perth Amboy

RARITAN RIVER

Princeton

Red Bank

95

Long Branch

PENNSYLVANIA

95

☆ **Trenton**

Asbury Park

195

295

ATLANTIC OCEAN

Philadelphia

76

Camden

New Jersey Turnpike

Cherry Hill

PINE BARRENS

Garden State Parkway

Wilmington

295

MULLICA RIVER

Vineland

GREAT EGG HARBOR RIVER

MAURICE RIVER

Edwin B. Forsythe National Wildlife Refuge

Atlantic City

DELAWARE

Delaware Bay

DID YOU KNOW?

that it's illegal to pump your own gasoline at service stations in New Jersey?

Cape May

57 miles (92 km)

ABOUT NEW JERSEY

NICKNAME: Garden State
CAPITAL: Trenton
STATEHOOD: December 18, 1787 (3rd)
MOTTO: Liberty and prosperity.

POPULATION: 8,484,431 (9th)
AREA: 8,722 sq. mi. (47th)
(22,580 sq km)
HIGHEST POINT: 1,803 ft. (High Point)
LOWEST POINT: Sea level (Atlantic Ocean)

FLOWER: Purple violet
TREE: Red oak
BIRD: Eastern goldfinch

New Jersey

Benjamin Franklin once described New Jersey as "a cider barrel tapped at both ends." He was referring to the fact that in colonial times New Jersey grew much of the food eaten in New York City and Philadelphia. Two centuries later, those cities still influence life in northern and southern New Jersey, respectively. Residents of the state's numerous suburbs often commute to jobs in New York City or Philadelphia, watch television stations emanating from those cities, and root for their major league sports teams.

Yet New Jersey has changed in many other ways. Most notably, it has transformed itself into an industrial powerhouse. For example, New Jersey leads the nation in pharmaceutical drug manufacturing and trails only Texas in chemical production. In addition, New Jersey boasts a number of important industrial research facilities—a tradition begun by Thomas Edison in 1876, when he built the first U.S. research laboratory in Menlo Park. Because of all this heavy industry, New Jersey has paid a steep price in toxic waste and environmental pollution. Recognizing this, a number of communities (especially Newark) have lately begun instituting promising clean-up programs.

Ironically, because so many New Jerseyans live crowded into suburbs, two thirds of the state is open land. In southern and eastern Jersey, this land is dominated by the Pine Barrens, a region of infertile soil sitting atop the Cohansey Aquifer, which is believed to hold the largest supply of freshwater in the Northeast.

The Jersey Shore begins at Cape May, the nation's first summer resort. A short drive north is Atlantic City, the home of the Miss America pageant since 1921 and legalized gambling since 1978. Closer to New York City are the beach towns made famous by Bruce Springsteen, who grew up near Asbury Park.

Among the states, New Jersey has the ninth largest population and the fourth smallest area. This means that a lot of New Jerseyans live in a relatively small space. As a result, New Jersey has the highest population density in the United States, with more people per square mile than India or Japan.

New Jersey's nickname is the Garden State because of its many truck farms. These small farms produce fresh vegetables, milk, and eggs that are shipped by truck to New York City and Philadelphia.

LEGEND

🛣️ 20	⭐	⬜	🌲🌲🌲	🔺	0 ⟶ miles 50	
Interstate Highways	State Capital	Native American Reservations	National Forests	Highest Point	0 ⟶ kilometers 80	

New York City is the hub of many industries, including fashion, theater, art, broadcasting, publishing, advertising, public relations, and financial services. New York City's financial community is collectively known as Wall Street because the New York Stock Exchange is located there.

CANADA

ST. LAWRENCE RIVER

St. Regis Reservation

Ogdensburg • Potsdam • Plattsburgh •

Lake Champlain

Lake Placid

• Burlington

RAQUETTE R.

Watertown •

ADIRONDACK MTS.

VERMONT

87

LAKE ONTARIO

81

Oswego •

Oneida Lake Rome •

Great Sacandaga Lake

Lake George

METTAWEE RIVER

Glens Falls •

ERIE CANAL

NIAGARA R.

• Niagara Falls

Rochester

Syracuse

Utica •

MOHAWK RIVER

90

Schenectady •

90

Geneva •

Finger Lakes

Oneonta •

88

Albany ⭐ • Troy

L. ERIE

Buffalo

90

390

• Ithaca

81

Corning •

Elmira •

SUSQUEHANNA R.

Binghamton •

CATSKILL MTS.

HUDSON RIVER

MASS.

90

GENESEE RIVER

Cattaraugus Reservation

Jamestown •

ALLEGHENY R.

Ashokan Reservoir

Kingston •

Poughkeepsie •

DELAWARE R.

87

CONN.

84

Allegany Reservation

PENNSYLVANIA

Scranton •

Newburgh •

Middletown •

684

95

Long Island Sound

Yonkers •

New York City •

Allentown •

N.J.

278

• Levittown

Hempstead

495

Riverhead

ATLANTIC OCEAN

• Trenton

DID YOU KNOW?

that in 1644 the governor of New York (then New Amsterdam) noted eighteen languages being spoken by the colony's inhabitants?

320 miles (515 km)

ABOUT NEW YORK

NICKNAME: Empire State

CAPITAL: Albany

STATEHOOD: July 26, 1788 (11th)

MOTTO: Ever upward.

POPULATION: 19,011,378 (3rd)

AREA: 54,471 sq. mi. (27th)
(141,019 sq km)

HIGHEST POINT: 5,344 ft. (Mount Marcy)

LOWEST POINT: Sea level (Atlantic Ocean)

FLOWER: Rose

TREE: Sugar maple

BIRD: Bluebird

FISH: Brook trout

New York

Until the late 1960s, New York State led the nation in nearly every economic, population, and cultural category. Now it ranks third in population and seventh in manufacturing jobs. New York's economic decline has particularly troubled upstate cities such as Buffalo and Rochester, which have lost thousands of high-paying industrial jobs. On the other hand, New York City remains essentially unchanged: It continues to be an international cultural center, the home of the world's most important financial markets, and the headquarters of more major corporations than anywhere else.

A clear distinction exists between residents of "the City" and the rest of the state's population. Manhattanites tend to think of upstate New York as nearly unpopulated, while many upstaters would probably consider New York City a foreign land if it didn't share the same state government. In fact, a remarkable number of languages are spoken in New York City, which has long been an important point of entry for immigrants.

Just as New York State's people and economy are highly diverse, so is its geography. The only state to border both the Atlantic Ocean and the Great Lakes, New York encompasses nine topographical regions, most created by glaciers during the last Ice Age. The state's two major mountain ranges are the Catskills and the Adirondacks. The Adirondacks are particularly notable because the state has set aside a large portion of these rugged, sparsely populated mountains as a wilderness preserve.

The Melting Pot

Although most cities in New York have varied populations, none compares with New York City for its racial, religious, and ethnic mix. For instance, in New York City, there are significant populations of Puerto Ricans, Dominicans, Haitians, Mexicans, Jews, and Chinese. In addition, there are more blacks in New York than in any other state.

Buffalo gets more attention, but Syracuse is actually the snowiest U.S. city outside Alaska, with a mean annual snowfall of 110.1 inches (279.7 cm). The reason is the lake effect. As air moves west, it soaks up moisture over the Great Lakes. When this air reaches land and cools down, the excess moisture is squeezed out as snow.

In the Hudson River Valley, although apples are an important crop, milk is the leading agricultural commodity. Statewide, dairy products account for about half of all farm income.

LEGEND

🛣 20 Interstate Highways	⭐ State Capital	⬛ National Parks and Refuges	🌲 National Forests	🔺 Highest Point	0 miles 50 / 0 kilometers 80

DID YOU KNOW?

that Pittsburgh's steel factories once produced so much smoke that motorists had to use headlights during the day?

LAKE ERIE

NEW YORK

Erie ● 90

Erie National Wildlife Refuge

Binghamton

90

OHIO

Pymatuning Reservoir 79

Bradford

ALLEGHENY RIVER

81 Lake Wallenpaupack

DELAWARE RIVER

84

● Oil City

WEST BRANCH SUSQUEHANNA R.

Williamsport

Scranton

Wilkes-Barre ●

380

80

Youngstown

80

● New Castle

180

80

Hazleton ●

80

● Butler

76

State College

80

81

N.J.

ALLEGHENY MTS.

Pottsville ●

Bethlehem

76

OHIO R.

JUNIATA R.

78

95 Trenton

Pittsburgh

● Altoona

Harrisburg ⭐

Reading

Allentown

Johnstown

99

Hershey

SCHUYLKILL R.

276

Greensburg

MONONGAHELA R.

Raystown Lake

76

Lancaster

SUSQUEHANNA R.

95

70

76

Carlisle

Philadelphia ●

79

Chambersburg

York

83

Chester ●

70

81

● Wilmington

95

W. VA.

VA.

MARYLAND

DEL.

Baltimore ●

Lancaster County in the heart of Pennsylvania Dutch country has a high concentration of dairy farms. That's why Milton Hershey chose to locate his milk chocolate business there. Since Hershey's factory opened in 1905, it has grown to become the world's largest chocolate plant.

◄————— 307 miles (494 km) —————►

ABOUT PENNSYLVANIA

NICKNAME: Keystone State

CAPITAL: Harrisburg

STATEHOOD: December 12, 1787 (2nd)

MOTTO: Virtue, liberty, and independence.

POPULATION: 12,287,150 (6th)

AREA: 46,058 sq. mi. (33rd) (119,239 sq km)

HIGHEST POINT: 3,213 ft. (Mount Davis)

LOWEST POINT: Sea level (Delaware River)

FLOWER: Mountain laurel

TREE: Hemlock

BIRD: Ruffed grouse

FISH: Brook trout

Pennsylvania

Like neighboring West Virginia, Pennsylvania is a coal state. Its plentiful energy resources once fueled major steel factories in Pittsburgh, Allentown, and elsewhere. Now with most of those mills closed, the air is cleaner, but some local economies have yet to recover.

Easing that economic burden has been the state's robust food-processing industry. Pennsylvania leads the nation in the production of snack foods, especially potato chips, pretzels, and chocolate. It also ranks fourth in milk production and fourth in ice cream making.

Without all this agriculture, the cities of Philadelphia (the fifth largest in the nation by population) and Pittsburgh (the fifty-second largest by population) might otherwise dominate the state. Instead, the character of Pennsylvania has remained largely rural, with values and interests to match. The two most popular pastimes in western Pennsylvania, for example, are high school football and deer hunting.

Overall, mountains and rivers dominate the landscape, particularly atop the Appalachian Plateau covering northern and western Pennsylvania. In the southeastern corner of the state, across the Allegheny Mountains, a stretch of the Piedmont underlies the fertile farmland of Pennsylvania Dutch country. Beyond lies Philadelphia, perched on a tiny strip of the Atlantic Coastal Plain. Philadelphia and Erie, the state's two most important ports, give Pennsylvania access to both the Atlantic Ocean (via the Delaware River) and the Great Lakes.

Pennsylvania has more than a million licensed hunters of all ages. When its two-week buck-hunting season begins on the first Monday after Thanksgiving, cities across the state become ghost towns. Schools close and businesses run short of help as up to one third of a town's population heads for the woods.

During the nineteenth century, many Amish and Mennonite farmers settled in Lancaster County. Because they came from Germany (and not Holland), one might wonder why they're called the Pennsylvania Dutch. The reason is that the German word for "German" is *Deutsch,* which looks and sounds like *Dutch.*

Three Rivers
At Pittsburgh, once the nation's busiest inland port, the Allegheny and Monongahela rivers meet to form the Ohio. The Ohio River then flows southwest, joining the Mississippi at Cairo, Illinois.

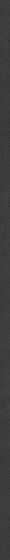

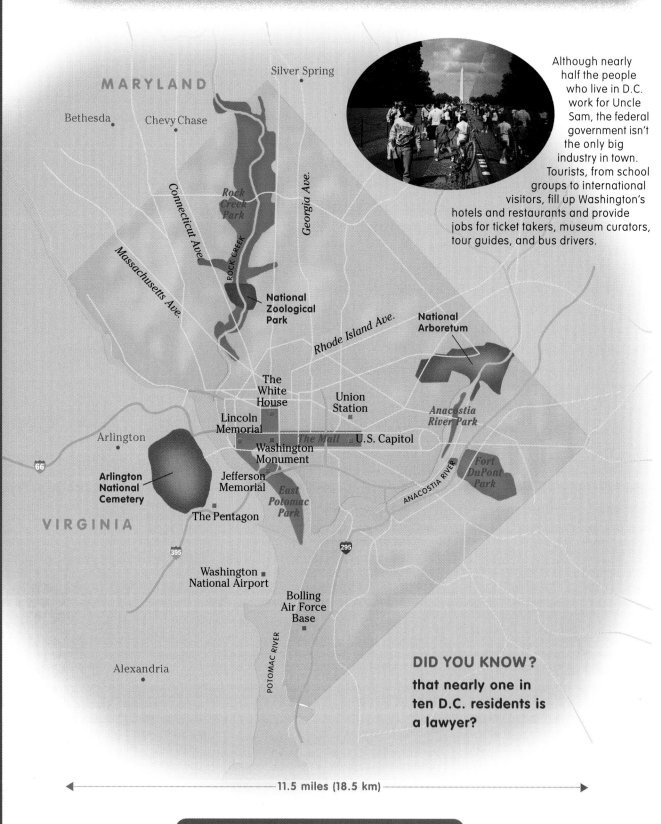

Interstate Highways

National Parks and Refuges

Public Parks

Places of Interest

| 0 | miles | 2 |
| 0 | kilometers | 3.2 |

MARYLAND

Silver Spring

Bethesda

Chevy Chase

Connecticut Ave.

Rock Creek Park

ROCK CREEK

Georgia Ave.

Massachusetts Ave.

National Zoological Park

Rhode Island Ave.

National Arboretum

The White House

Union Station

Anacostia River Park

Lincoln Memorial

The Mall

U.S. Capitol

Arlington

Washington Monument

Jefferson Memorial

East Potomac Park

ANACOSTIA RIVER

Fort DuPont Park

Arlington National Cemetery

The Pentagon

66

VIRGINIA

395

295

Washington National Airport

Bolling Air Force Base

POTOMAC RIVER

Alexandria

Although nearly half the people who live in D.C. work for Uncle Sam, the federal government isn't the only big industry in town. Tourists, from school groups to international visitors, fill up Washington's hotels and restaurants and provide jobs for ticket takers, museum curators, tour guides, and bus drivers.

DID YOU KNOW?

that nearly one in ten D.C. residents is a lawyer?

←——————— 11.5 miles (18.5 km) ———————→

ABOUT WASHINGTON, D.C.

NICKNAME: __

CAPITAL: __

STATEHOOD: __

MOTTO: Justice for all.

POPULATION: 571,822

AREA: 68 sq. mi.

(176 sq km)

HIGHEST POINT: 410 ft. (Tenleytown)

LOWEST POINT: 1 ft. (Potomac River)

FLOWER: American Beauty rose

TREE: Scarlet oak

BIRD: Wood thrush

Washington, D.C.

Each year, nearly twenty million people visit the District of Columbia. They come to see the White House, the Smithsonian Institution, and other popular tourist attractions. The grandeur of Washington's public architecture and the elegance of its street plan have led many to compare the city favorably with the most gracious European capitals. Yet when travelers arrive, they cannot help but find another Washington existing within the nation's capital, a troubled city in which poverty obscures all the wealth, privilege, and influence.

Until 1974, congressional committees governed the district. Then, in response to public pressure, Congress passed the Home Rule Act establishing a locally elected government. Sadly, this government functioned poorly. Crime rates rose, and streets became potholed, causing Congress to take back control of most city functions in 1995.

D.C. residents, two thirds of whom are black, have no voting representative in Congress because the district isn't part of any state. (The land was given to the federal government by Maryland in 1791.) However, D.C. residents do benefit greatly from the presence of the federal government, which provides hundreds of thousands of jobs and creates many other business opportunities. The presence of so many foreign embassies and international organizations also makes Washington a remarkably cosmopolitan place to live.

Originally, Washington was just one city within the District of Columbia. Today, it fills the entire district, and its metro area extends well beyond into the neighboring suburbs of Maryland and Virginia.

Many American cities suffer from urban problems such as crime and homelessness. In Washington, D.C., those problems have been particularly severe. For example, D.C. schools have a dropout rate close to 40 percent, the highest in the nation, and the poverty there can resemble that of an underdeveloped country.

When it was first surveyed in 1791, the District of Columbia formed a square ten miles (16 km) on each side, including land on both banks of the Potomac. In 1846, however, the federal government gave Virginia back its land, reducing the district's size from one hundred to sixty-eight square miles (259 to 176 sq km).

George Washington had the new federal city built at the head of navigation of the Potomac River— that is, at the point beyond which ships couldn't sail upstream because of rapids and waterfalls.

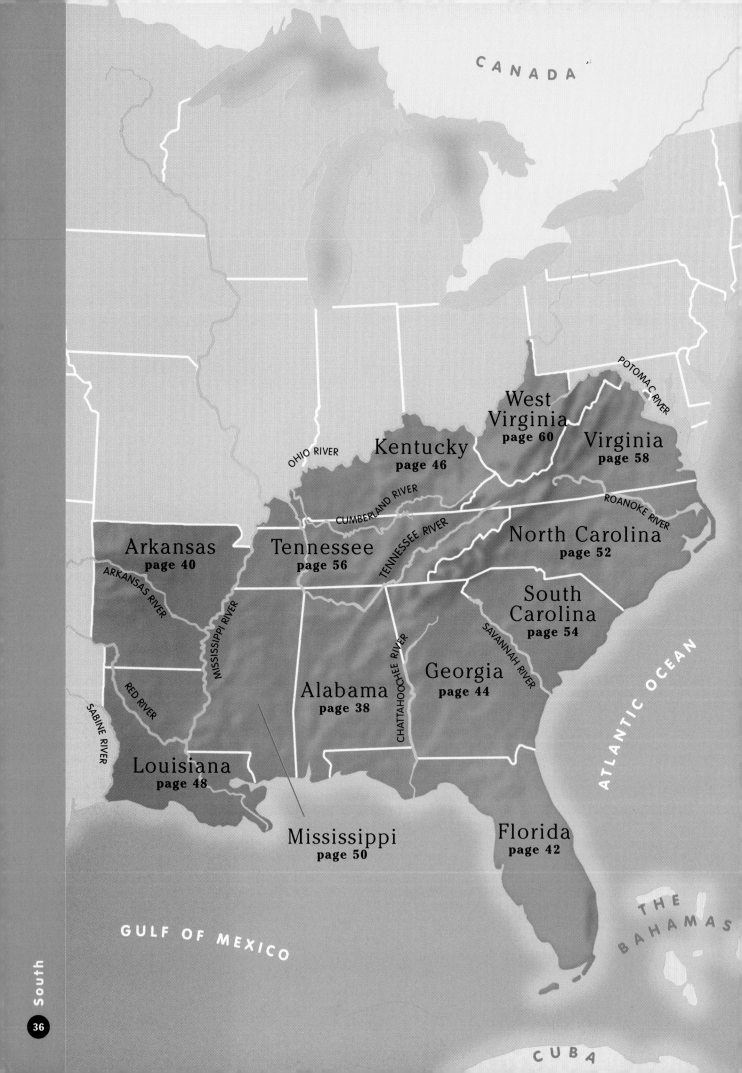

CANADA

POTOMAC RIVER

West
Virginia
page 60

Virginia
page 58

OHIO RIVER

Kentucky
page 46

ROANOKE RIVER

CUMBERLAND RIVER

North Carolina
page 52

Arkansas
page 40

Tennessee
page 56

TENNESSEE RIVER

ARKANSAS RIVER

South
Carolina
page 54

MISSISSIPPI RIVER

SAVANNAH RIVER

RED RIVER

Alabama
page 38

CHATTAHOOCHEE RIVER

Georgia
page 44

ATLANTIC OCEAN

SABINE RIVER

Louisiana
page 48

Mississippi
page 50

Florida
page 42

THE
BAHAMAS

GULF OF MEXICO

CUBA

For geographical purposes, it sometimes makes sense to divide the southern states into three groups. Virginia, the Carolinas, Georgia, and Florida make up the seaboard states. With the exception of Florida, they all slope down from the Appalachian Mountains through the Piedmont to the Atlantic Coastal Plain. On the other hand, much of Alabama, Mississippi, Louisiana, and Arkansas is bottomland, enriched by the annual flooding of rivers such as the Mississippi. Finally, Tennessee, Kentucky, and West Virginia sit atop the rugged Appalachian highlands.

South

LEGEND

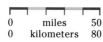

Interstate Highways	State Capital	Native American Reservations	National Forests	Highest Point	0 miles 50 0 kilometers 80

Rocket City, U.S.A.

In 1960, the National Aeronautics and Space Administration (NASA) opened the George C. Marshall Space Flight Center in Huntsville. Since then, many highly trained engineers from around the country have moved to Huntsville to work for the numerous rocketry companies now located there.

DID YOU KNOW?

that half of all U.S. peanuts are grown within one hundred miles (161 km) of Dothan, the self-styled Peanut Capital of the World?

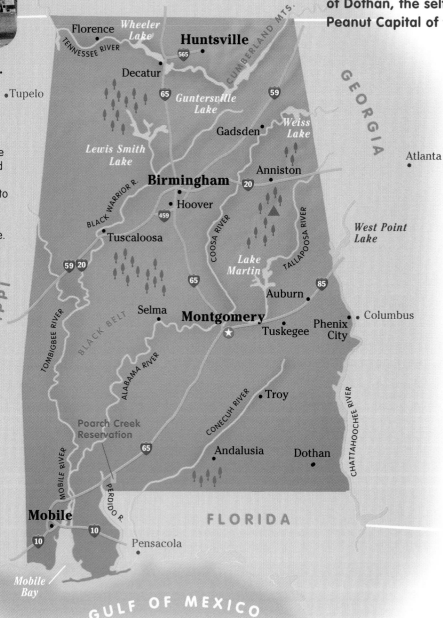

TENNESSEE

Florence
Wheeler Lake
Huntsville
TENNESSEE RIVER
565
CUMBERLAND MTS.
Tupelo
Decatur
65
Guntersville Lake
59
GEORGIA
Gadsden
Weiss Lake
Lewis Smith Lake
BLACK WARRIOR R.
Birmingham
Anniston
Atlanta
20
Hoover
COOSA RIVER
TALLAPOOSA RIVER
459
West Point Lake
Tuscaloosa
Lake Martin
59 20
65
Auburn
85
MISSISSIPPI
Selma
BLACK BELT
Montgomery
Tuskegee
Phenix City
Columbus
TOMBIGBEE RIVER
ALABAMA RIVER
CONECUH RIVER
Troy
CHATTAHOOCHEE RIVER
Poarch Creek Reservation
65
Andalusia
Dothan
MOBILE RIVER
PERDIDO R.
Mobile
FLORIDA
10
10
Pensacola
Mobile Bay

GULF OF MEXICO

189 miles (304 km)

ABOUT ALABAMA

NICKNAME: Heart of Dixie

CAPITAL: Montgomery

STATEHOOD: December 14, 1819 (22nd)

MOTTO: We dare defend our rights.

POPULATION: 4,464,356 (23rd)

AREA: 52,423 sq. mi. (30th)
(135,717 sq km)

HIGHEST POINT: 2,405 ft. (Cheaha Mountain)

LOWEST POINT: Sea level (Gulf of Mexico)

FLOWER: Camellia

TREE: Southern pine

BIRD: Yellowhammer

FISH: Largemouth bass, tarpon

Alabama

Which changed Alabama more: the Civil War or the boll weevil? Don't answer too quickly. Even after the Civil War, cotton farming continued to dominate the economy, while blacks still suffered from segregation and worse. Then, in 1915, an insect pest called the boll weevil infested Alabama's cotton fields. At the same time, the steel factories in Birmingham began to boom, offering jobs that lured many farm families from the countryside to the city. Together, the boll weevil and the steel jobs urbanized and industrialized what had been a thoroughly rural state.

Today in Alabama, steel, like cotton, has faded in importance, yet new manufacturing industries have taken its place. Paper mills, for example, thrive in Mobile and Montgomery, which makes sense for Alabama because forests cover two-thirds of the state. Culturally, though, many Alabamans prefer to revere the past, proudly maintaining many traditions commonly associated with the Old South. Some of these are positive, such as the leisurely pace of life, especially during the region's long, hot summers; others reflect problems that still need to be solved, such as the lingering poverty in the countryside.

Although it's difficult to tell from the ground, Alabama is tilted like a washboard. From the state's northeastern corner, where the Appalachian Mountains begin, the land slopes gradually down to the south and west. Following the land, most of Alabama's rivers flow southwest into Mobile Bay.

Traditions are important in Alabama, where most residents can trace their roots back to the nineteenth century. In the black community, which makes up one-fourth of the state, churches have been particularly active in social and political causes. Martin Luther King, Jr., for example, began his ministerial career at the Dexter Avenue Baptist Church in Montgomery (pictured above).

Limestone

Coal

Iron Ore

The key raw materials used in making iron and steel are iron ore, coal, and limestone. Alabama is the only place in the world where these three ingredients can be found within a ten-mile (sixteen-kilometer) radius.

Millions of years ago, the Gulf of Mexico covered southern Alabama. When it receded, it left behind a strip of rich, dark soil called the Black Belt. Once home to grand cotton plantations, the Black Belt now provides pastureland for cattle.

LEGEND

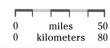 Interstate Highways

 State Capital

National Parks and Refuges

National Forests

▲ Highest Point

| 0 | miles | 50 |
| 0 | kilometers | 80 |

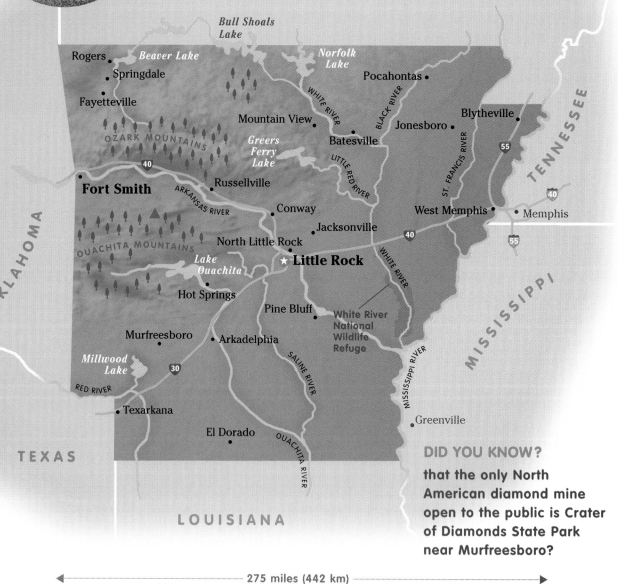

Even though Arkansas farmers produce nearly half of the nation's rice, the state's most important agricultural product is the broiler chicken. (Broilers are young chickens about seven weeks old.) Arkansas-based Tyson Foods, the world's largest poultry company, processes about forty million birds each week.

MISSOURI

Bull Shoals Lake

Rogers
Beaver Lake
Springdale
Norfolk Lake
Fayetteville
Pocahontas
Blytheville
WHITE RIVER
BLACK RIVER
Mountain View
Jonesboro
Batesville
OZARK MOUNTAINS
Greers Ferry Lake
ST. FRANCIS RIVER
LITTLE RED RIVER
Russellville
Fort Smith
ARKANSAS RIVER
Conway
West Memphis
Memphis
Jacksonville
North Little Rock
★ Little Rock
OUACHITA MOUNTAINS
Lake Ouachita
WHITE RIVER
Hot Springs
Pine Bluff
White River National Wildlife Refuge
Murfreesboro
Arkadelphia
Millwood Lake
SALINE RIVER
RED RIVER
Texarkana
MISSISSIPPI RIVER
El Dorado
Greenville
OUACHITA RIVER

OKLAHOMA

TEXAS

TENNESSEE

MISSISSIPPI

LOUISIANA

DID YOU KNOW?

that the only North American diamond mine open to the public is Crater of Diamonds State Park near Murfreesboro?

◄─────── 275 miles (442 km) ───────►

ABOUT ARKANSAS

NICKNAME: Natural State

CAPITAL: Little Rock

STATEHOOD: June 15, 1836 (25th)

MOTTO: The people rule.

POPULATION: 2,692,090 (33rd)

AREA: 53,182 sq. mi. (29th)
(137,682 sq km)

HIGHEST POINT: 2,753 ft. (Magazine Mt.)

LOWEST POINT: 55 ft. (Ouachita River)

FLOWER: Apple blossom

TREE: Pine

BIRD: Mockingbird

Arkansas

Little Rock, the state capital, is more than Arkansas's economic and political hub: It's very nearly the wheel itself. Outside this modern city, the rest of the state is mostly countryside. In many towns, people live so far apart that there is no Main Street or downtown shopping area. Although tourism has brought many visitors to Arkansas in recent years, the people who live there have changed remarkably little. Nearly 99 percent of them were born in the United States, and more than two thirds were born in Arkansas itself. As a result, the state's population, though racially mixed, isn't culturally diverse.

A diagonal line drawn across Arkansas from the northeast to the southwest would separate the state's lowlands from its highlands. Above this line, which would pass through Little Rock, would be two mountain ranges: the Ouachitas and the Ozarks. The Ouachitas are known for their hot springs, which Native Americans visited for thousands of years before white settlers arrived. The isolated Ozark Plateau features broad ridges and deep valleys cut by fast-moving streams. Separating these ranges is the Arkansas River Valley. Like nearly every river in the state, the Arkansas flows southeast and empties into the Mississippi.

Pine forests cover much of the Arkansas lowlands, yet near the Mississippi River the land has been cleared to allow farming. Once the warm, moist soil produced large harvests of cotton. Now soybeans and rice are the most profitable crops.

During the 1960s, when new roads were built in the Ozarks to encourage tourism, the region became less isolated but also lost some of its individuality. Now the Ozark Folk Center in Mountain View preserves many fading traditions of the mountain people, including their music and crafts such as wood carving and quilt making.

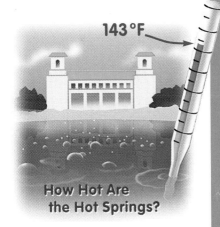

143°F

How Hot Are the Hot Springs?

Two million people a year visit the resort town of Hot Springs on the eastern edge of the Ouachita Mountains. Most go to bathe in the naturally hot mineral water that bubbles from the ground there at 143°F (62°C). According to local Native American tradition, this water is warmed by the breath of the Great Spirit.

The dense pine and hardwood forests that cover the Ozark Plateau once made travel difficult. In this way, the terrain contributed to the isolation of the people who lived there.

LEGEND

Interstate Highways	State Capital	National Parks and Refuges	Marshlands	Highest Point	0 miles 50 0 kilometers 80

ALABAMA

Albany •

GEORGIA

Dothan •

Lake Seminole

• Valdosta

PERDIDO RIVER

ESCAMBIA RIVER

ST. MARYS RIVER

ATLANTIC OCEAN

Pensacola

APALACHICOLA R.

Tallahassee

Jacksonville

Panama City •

St. Augustine

ST. JOHNS R.

SUWANNEE RIVER

Gainesville

DID YOU KNOW?

that St. Augustine is the oldest continuously occupied European settlement in the United States?

Lake George

Daytona Beach

Ocala

GULF OF MEXICO

Orlando •

Cape Canaveral

John F. Kennedy Space Center

Tampa

Clearwater •

Lakeland

Melbourne

Lake Kissimmee

Palm Bay

St. Petersburg

KISSIMMEE R.

Sarasota •

Port St. Lucie

Port Charlotte

Lake Okeechobee

West Palm Beach

Fort Myers

Coral Springs

Boca Raton

Pompano Beach

Fort Lauderdale

Hollywood

Naples

Hialeah

Miami Beach

Miami

Biscayne Bay

Kendall

Everglades National Park

The most important industry in Florida is tourism. For many years, northern "snowbirds" have wintered in the Sunshine State. Now tourism flourishes during summer, too. Walt Disney World near Orlando, for example, is among the top five tourist attractions in the world.

Florida Bay

Key Largo

Florida Keys

Key West •   Marathon

—————— 361 miles (581 km) ——————

ABOUT FLORIDA

NICKNAME: Sunshine State
CAPITAL: Tallahassee
STATEHOOD: March 3, 1845 (27th)
MOTTO: In God we trust.

POPULATION: 16,396,515 (4th)
AREA: 65,756 sq. mi. (22nd)
(170,234 sq km)
HIGHEST POINT: 345 ft. (Walton County)
LOWEST POINT: Sea level (Atlantic Ocean)

FLOWER: Orange blossom
TREE: Sabal palm
BIRD: Mockingbird

South • Florida

42

Florida

The typically warm, sunny weather in Florida affects nearly every aspect of life there. Nearly seventy million tourists a year visit the state to enjoy its tropical climate, and the plentiful sunshine also attracts many retirees. In fact, so many older Americans have moved to Florida, the southernmost of the continental states, that it now has the highest percentage of residents over age sixty-five of any state. Another factor contributing to the diversity of Florida's population is immigration, particularly the arrival of many Cuban and Haitian refugees. Overall, Florida has one of the lowest percentages of residents who were born in the state.

Many of the newcomers, especially the well-to-do retirees, live in condominiums lining the bone-white Gold Coast beaches between Miami and West Palm Beach. The Florida Keys, small limestone-and-coral islands off the state's southern tip, are another chic resort area. Northern Florida, however, is predominantly rural, resembling its neighbors Alabama and Georgia much more than it resembles urban, Latin-flavored Miami.

Finally, Florida is the flattest state. Its highest point, in the Panhandle near the Alabama border, is 345 feet (105 m) above sea level. Farther south, on the peninsula separating the Atlantic Ocean from the Gulf of Mexico, the average elevation is less than 100 feet (30 m) above sea level.

Florida's Spanish Accent
In 1513, Spanish explorer Juan Ponce de León became the first European to discover Florida. Since then, Hispanic culture has been an important part of Florida's architecture, cuisine, and lifestyle. Today, most Spanish-speaking Floridians live in and around Miami, where many Cubans have settled.

The orchards of central Florida dominate U.S. citrus production. About 80 percent of the nation's oranges and grapefruit are grown in the state, where nine out of every ten oranges are used to make orange juice.

Florida's most unusual topographical feature, and one of the country's most important wildlife refuges, is the Everglades. Although most people think of the Everglades as a swamp, it's actually a shallow river fifty miles (80 km) wide that carries overflow from Lake Okeechobee into Florida Bay. Its average depth is six inches (15 cm).

LEGEND

 Interstate Highways

 State Capital

National Parks and Refuges

National Forests

Marshlands

Highest Point

| 0 | miles | 50 |
| 0 | kilometers | 80 |

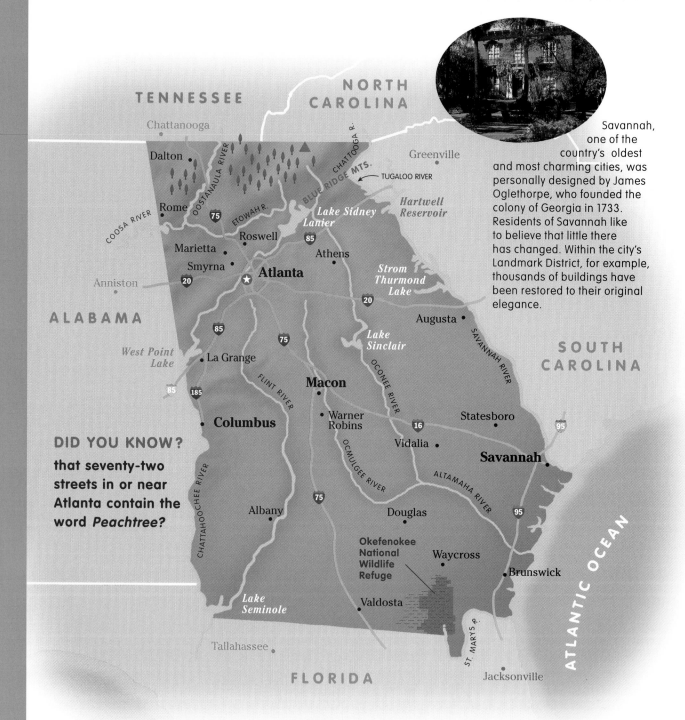

Savannah, one of the country's oldest and most charming cities, was personally designed by James Oglethorpe, who founded the colony of Georgia in 1733. Residents of Savannah like to believe that little there has changed. Within the city's Landmark District, for example, thousands of buildings have been restored to their original elegance.

DID YOU KNOW?

that seventy-two streets in or near Atlanta contain the word *Peachtree?*

254 miles (409 km)

ABOUT GEORGIA

NICKNAME: Empire State of the South

CAPITAL: Atlanta

STATEHOOD: January 2, 1788 (4th)

MOTTO: Wisdom, justice, moderation.

POPULATION: 8,383,915 (10th)

AREA: 59,441 sq. mi. (24th)
(153,886 sq km)

HIGHEST POINT: 4,784 ft. (Brasstown Bald)

LOWEST POINT: Sea level (Atlantic Ocean)

FLOWER: Cherokee rose

TREE: Live oak

BIRD: Brown thrasher

FISH: Largemouth bass

Georgia

At one time a cotton state like its neighbors, Georgia now finds itself at the head of the New South, the name given to those states in the region that have successfully updated their economies. The key has been diversification. Today, cotton makes up just 8 percent of Georgia's farm income, with peanuts, pecans, and peaches gaining in importance. (Georgia now leads the nation in all three of these crops). The state also ranks high in the production of granite, marble, wood pulp, aircraft, textiles, and the fine china clays used to make dinnerware.

Another important step in Georgia's economic revival was the civil rights movement of the 1960s, which pushed the state to become more progressive and cosmopolitan. White Georgians learned to work with, not against, blacks, who make up more than one quarter of the population. Some black Georgians still live on farms, yet many more have moved to the cities, particularly Atlanta, where a strong black middle class has emerged.

In northern Georgia, the Blue Ridge Mountains dot the landscape with "balds," or treeless hilltops. From Atlanta southward, however, the belly of the state sits on the rolling Piedmont Plateau, which itself slopes down to the wetlands of the Atlantic and Gulf coastal plains. Along the Florida border is the huge Okefenokee Swamp, one of the nation's leading bird refuges. In the language of the Seminole, *okefenokee* means "land of the trembling earth."

Any item of woven or knit cloth is generally called a textile. Although Georgia trails North Carolina in overall textile production, it leads the nation in carpet making. The center of this industry is the Dalton area, which produces 80 percent of the nation's carpeting.

Atlanta, the acknowledged capital of the New South, has been sucking up Georgians like a vacuum cleaner. At least two out of every five now live within the Atlanta metropolitan area, which has become the most important commercial, financial, and transportation center south of Washington, D.C., and east of Dallas.

Georgia's Piedmont Plateau is known for its red clay hills. "I have a dream," Atlanta native Martin Luther King, Jr., said in his famous speech, "that one day on the red hills of Georgia, sons of former slaves and the sons of former slave owners will be able to sit down together at the table of brotherhood."

LEGEND

 Interstate Highways

 State Capital

■ National Parks and Refuges

National Forests

▲ Highest Point

| 0 | miles | 50 |
| 0 | kilometers | 80 |

Most Kentucky coal is strip-mined by power shovels that tear away the surface layer of trees, rocks, and soil. Because strip mining can pollute streams and destroy animal habitats, Kentuckians often have to choose between a healthy economy and a healthy ecology.

OHIO

Cincinnati
Covington
OHIO RIVER

INDIANA

Ashland

LICKING RIVER

BIG SANDY R.

Louisville   **Frankfort** ★
Fort Knox   **Lexington**

ILLINOIS

Evansville

Henderson
Owensboro
Radcliff
Richmond
W. VA.
TUG FORK RIVER

GREEN RIVER
Rosine
Elizabethtown
Danville
Berea
Pikeville
KENTUCKY R.

Madisonville
Mammoth Cave National Park
Somerset

OHIO RIVER

Cairo
Paducah
Lake Barkley
Bowling Green
BARREN R.
Lake Cumberland
VA.

MO.
MISSISSIPPI R.
TENNESSEE R.
Hopkinsvillle
CUMBERLAND MTS.

Kentucky Lake

CUMBERLAND RIVER

Nashville

TENNESSEE

Knoxville

N.C.

DID YOU KNOW ?

that bluegrass gets its name from the tiny bluish blossoms that the green grass produces each May?

◀------------ 350 miles (563 km) ------------▶

ABOUT KENTUCKY

NICKNAME: Bluegrass State

CAPITAL: Frankfort

STATEHOOD: June 1, 1792 (15th)

MOTTO: United we stand, divided we fall.

POPULATION: 4,065,556 (25th)

AREA: 40,411 sq. mi. (37th)
(104,619 sq km)

HIGHEST POINT: 4,139 ft. (Black Mountain)

LOWEST POINT: 257 ft. (Mississippi River)

FLOWER: Goldenrod

TREE: Tulip tree

BIRD: Kentucky cardinal

FISH: Bass

Kentucky

More so than other states, Kentucky is both rich and poor, beautiful and ugly. Its many waterways are among the most scenic in the nation, but elsewhere strip mining for coal has scarred the landscape. Similarly, great wealth exists alongside enduring poverty. In the Cumberland coalfields, labor unions have struggled for decades, sometimes violently, to raise unfairly low wages and improve dangerous working conditions. Yet not too far away, Lexington's immaculate horse farms recall the splendor and gentility of the pre–Civil War South.

Although the Kentucky economy has diversified in recent years—adding automobile plants, for example—it continues to depend on two traditional exports: coal and tobacco. Kentucky ranks second in tobacco behind North Carolina and third in coal behind Wyoming and West Virginia. Other notable Kentucky products are bourbon whiskey and grass seed.

Six major geographical regions cover the state: The coal-rich Cumberland Plateau, part of the Appalachian chain, dominates eastern Kentucky. In the north, surrounding Lexington, are the rolling fields of the Bluegrass. Enclosing the Bluegrass is a horseshoe-shaped line of hills called the Knobs, to the south and west of which lies the flat fertile Pennyroyal. Along the Ohio River are the Western Coal Fields, while in the southwestern corner is the Jackson Purchase, an area bounded by the Mississippi, Tennessee, and Ohio rivers and named after Andrew Jackson, who helped buy it from the Chickasaw in 1818.

Bluegrass, the folk music of this predominantly rural state, resembles old-time string-band music, except that it's faster, higher pitched, and more strident. Bill Monroe, who grew up in Rosine, developed the bluegrass style after World War II. Bluegrass features mandolins, fiddles, and especially banjos.

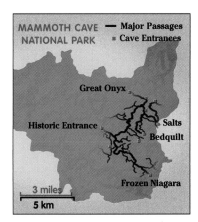

Beneath the Pennyroyal near Bowling Green is Mammoth Cave, the largest known cave system in the world. Its maze of tunnels and chambers was formed over millions of years by water trickling through limestone bedrock. So far, explorers have charted more than 350 miles (560 km) of tunnels on five underground levels.

The Bluegrass region provides nearly ideal conditions for raising thorough-bred racehorses. The lush grass on which these horses feed absorbs calcium from the limestone bedrock. This calcium promotes strong bones and muscles. The best thoroughbreds compete each May in the Kentucky Derby, run at the Churchill Downs racetrack in Louisville.

LEGEND

🛣 20	⭐	■	🌲	≈	▲	0 miles 50		
Interstate Highways	State Capital	National Parks and Refuges	National Forests	Marshlands	Highest Point	0 kilometers 80		

Texarkana

ARKANSAS

Caddo Lake

Lake Claiborne

Lake Bayou D'Arbonne

Shreveport
🛣 20
• Bossier City

Monroe 20

Vicksburg

RED RIVER

OUACHITA RIVER

TENSAS RIVER

MISSISSIPPI

Catahoula Lake

• Natchez

BLACK R.

Toledo Bend Reservoir

Alexandria

TEXAS

• De Ridder

49

ATCHAFALAYA R.

MISSISSIPPI RIVER

55

PEARL RIVER

Baton Rouge
⭐
10

12

12

59

DID YOU KNOW?

that because the early French and Spanish rulers of Louisiana were all Catholics, the state is divided into parishes rather than counties?

Lake Charles
10

• Lafayette

Beaumont

Sabine National Wildlife Refuge

Calcasieu Lake

Grand Lake

New Iberia

White Lake

Six Mile Lake

Lake Maurepas
10
55

Lake Pontchartrain

Slidell

Kenner
Metairie

New Orleans
10

Houma

MISSISSIPPI RIVER

GULF OF MEXICO

Offshore oil and gas exploration was pioneered off the coast of Louisiana. The state is currently the nation's fourth leading petroleum producer (behind Texas, Alaska, and California) and its second leading producer of natural gas (behind Texas).

⟵ 237 miles (381 km) ⟶

ABOUT LOUISIANA

NICKNAME: Pelican State
CAPITAL: Baton Rouge
STATEHOOD: April 30, 1812 (18th)
MOTTO: Union, justice, confidence.

POPULATION: 4,465,430 (22nd)
AREA: 51,843 sq. mi. (31st)
(134,215 sq km)
HIGHEST POINT: 535 ft. (Driskill Mountain)
LOWEST POINT: -8 ft. (New Orleans)

FLOWER: Magnolia
TREE: Bald cypress
BIRD: Brown pelican

Louisiana

Before the United States purchased Louisiana in 1803, it had been both a French and a Spanish colony. There were also slaves in the territory, brought to work on the numerous cotton plantations. Over time, these three cultures merged to form what is today known as Creole.

The Cajuns, who live in Louisiana's southern bayous, also have French roots, yet they came to Louisiana by way of Canada. In 1755, the British expelled about ten thousand French colonists from Acadia (now Nova Scotia), and many made their way south to Louisiana. Lately, the national popularity of zydeco music has stimulated a resurgence of the Cajun French language and culture.

Blacks, who make up 32 percent of the population, were long denied economic and political power in Louisiana. Yet they made important cultural contributions. Jazz music, for example, was invented by black performers in New Orleans about 1900.

Although agriculture remains important in Louisiana, the state's economy now depends more on shipping, petroleum, and the chemical industry. Between Baton Rouge and New Orleans, the banks of the Mississippi River are lined with chemical plants and oil refineries. In general, the Mississippi dominates the physical geography of the state. The southern half of Louisiana is remarkably flat, with low-lying swamps and a beachless coastline. As one moves north, however, the land rises slowly to prairies and low hills.

Nothing shows off Louisiana's rich cultural mix so much as its cooking. The world-famous Creole cuisine of New Orleans is a distinctive yet elegant blend of French, Spanish, and African dishes. In bayou country, however, Cajuns favor much spicier food, such as gumbo (a stew) and jambalaya (a rice dish).

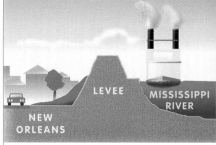

Rivers are constantly depositing sediment along their banks as well as on their bottoms. Sometimes this sediment builds up so high that the river rises to a level above that of the surrounding land. This has happened at New Orleans, where levees have been constructed to protect the city from flooding.

A bayou is a stream that moves slowly through marshland. The bayous of southern Louisiana provide important habitats for migrating birds, especially the wild ducks and geese that winter there.

LEGEND

🛣 20	⭐	⬛	🌲	⬛	🔺	0 miles 50	
Interstate Highways	State Capital	Native American Reservations	National Forests	National Parks and Refuges	Highest Point	0 kilometers 80	

TENNESSEE

Pickwick Lake

Memphis

Southaven Holly Springs

Sardis Lake

Oxford Tupelo

Clarksdale

55

YALOBUSHA R.

Grenada Lake

Cleveland

Greenwood Columbus

Greenville Starkville

BLACK PRAIRIE

Yazoo City

Ross Barnett Reservoir

Mississippi Choctaw Reservation

BIG BLACK RIVER

20 Meridian 20 59

Vicksburg **Jackson**

MISSISSIPPI RIVER

PEARL RIVER

Laurel

Natchez 55

Hattiesburg

Mississippi Sandhill Crane National Wildlife Refuge

59 Mobile

DID YOU KNOW?

that Mississippi Delta topsoil can be as deep as twenty-five feet (8 m) in some places?

Baton Rouge

Gulfport 10
Biloxi Pascagoula

New Orleans

GULF OF MEXICO

ARKANSAS

LOUISIANA

ALABAMA

TALLAHATCHIE R.

YAZOO RIVER

TENNESSEE HILLS

TOMBIGBEE RIVER

In Mississippi, many farmers have turned unproductive cotton fields into profitable catfish farms by flooding them. These aquaculturists fatten young catfish on grain before harvesting them, just as any farmer would fatten a cow or chicken before sending it to the slaughterhouse.

◄— 188 miles (302 km) —►

ABOUT MISSISSIPPI

NICKNAME: Magnolia State
CAPITAL: Jackson
STATEHOOD: December 10, 1817 (20th)
MOTTO: By valor and arms.

POPULATION: 2,858,029 (31st)
AREA: 48,434 sq. mi. (32nd)
(125,390 sq km)
HIGHEST POINT: 806 ft. (Woodall Mountain)
LOWEST POINT: Sea level (Gulf of Mexico)

FLOWER: Magnolia
TREE: Magnolia
BIRD: Mockingbird
FISH: Largemouth bass

Mississippi

Of all the states in the Union, Mississippi had the hardest time transitioning from the nineteenth century. The core of the problem was the poor relationship between whites and blacks. (Blacks in Mississippi make up 36 percent of the population, the highest percentage of any state.) The hostility that existed between these two groups from the Civil War until the 1960s virtually guaranteed that Mississippi would place last year after year in nearly every economic ranking. Yet the remarkable courage and wisdom shown by black Mississippians during the civil rights movement taught a majority of whites that keeping blacks down meant keeping Mississippi down as well. Since the 1970s, whites and blacks have worked together, and conditions in Mississippi have greatly improved.

Agriculture remains fundamental to the economy of this mainly rural state, yet manufacturing has become an increasingly vital part of the mix. In recent years, for example, many Mississippians have moved south to work in the shipyards at Pascagoula or for one of the oil and gas companies lining the Gulf Coast.

Although not as important economically as it once was, the Mississippi River remains the most important geographic feature in the state's flat landscape. The river's floodplain, a region known as the Delta, is quite narrow south of Vicksburg. In northern Mississippi, however, it widens to include the entire basin between the Mississippi and Yazoo rivers.

Faulkner Country
Mississippi has produced many great writers, including Eudora Welty, Tennessee Williams, and especially William Faulkner. Setting his books in small-town Mississippi, Faulkner made fictional Yoknapatawpha County one of the most celebrated locations in American literature. For the last thirty years of his life, Faulkner lived at Rowan Oak in Oxford (pictured above).

Most naturally occurring lakes in Mississippi are oxbows, formed by sudden changes in the course of the Mississippi River. Although the center of the river marks the state's boundary with Louisiana and Arkansas, land cut off from Mississippi by abrupt course changes still belongs to Mississippi.

The topsoil of the Mississippi Delta is particularly rich because for thousands of years annual flooding dumped tons and tons of silt over the land. Now artificial levees of earth, sand, rock, and concrete keep the river generally within its banks.

LEGEND

 Interstate Highways

 State Capital

Native American Reservations

National Forests

National Parks and Refuges

Marshlands

▲ Highest Point

| 0 | miles | 50 |
| 0 | km | 80 |

North Carolina leads the nation in the production of both tobacco and tobacco products, such as cigarettes. Tobacco fields blanket much of the Piedmont, where farmers have been reluctant to give up their way of life (and suffer financial hardship) even though tobacco has been shown to be a health hazard.

VIRGINIA

Buggs Island Lake

Virginia Beach

Great Smoky Mountains National Park

TENN.

CHOWAN R.

Lake Gaston

ROANOKE R.

85

BLUE RIDGE MOUNTAINS

YADKIN RIVER

77

Greensboro

Burlington

95

Winston-Salem

Durham

Knoxville

CATAWBA R.

High Point

Chapel Hill

Raleigh

Rocky Mount

40

Asheville

85

Cary

Wilson

26

Lake Norman

UHARIE R.

40

Greenville

Gastonia

Lake Tillery

Goldsboro

Cherokee Reservation

85

Charlotte

Fayetteville

NEUSE RIVER

40

Cape Hatteras

PEE DEE RIVER

77

95

Jacksonville

Cape Lookout

SOUTH CAROLINA

CAPE FEAR RIVER

GEORGIA

Columbia

Wilmington

Cape Fear

ATLANTIC OCEAN

DID YOU KNOW?

that North Carolina's Mount Mitchell is the highest point east of the Mississippi River?

◄———————— 503 miles (809 km) ————————►

ABOUT NORTH CAROLINA

NICKNAME: Tar Heel State

CAPITAL: Raleigh

STATEHOOD: November 21, 1789 (12th)

MOTTO: To be rather than to seem.

POPULATION: 8,186,268 (11th)

AREA: 53,821 sq. mi. (28th)
(139,336 sq km)

HIGHEST POINT: 6,684 ft. (Mount Mitchell)

LOWEST POINT: Sea level (Atlantic Ocean)

FLOWER: Flowering dogwood

TREE: Longleaf pine

BIRD: Cardinal

FISH: Channel bass

North Carolina

Most of North Carolina's major rivers begin along the state's western edge, where the Blue Ridge and Great Smoky mountains rise up to form the highest peaks in the long Appalachian chain. From these mountains, where the people practice handicrafts much as their ancestors did, the water flows east in narrow, swift-moving streams down to the Piedmont Plateau. That's where North Carolina's largest cities are located and where most of its money is made. On the busy Piedmont, furniture and textile manufacturers add considerably to the even larger profits of the tobacco industry.

Passing into the Tidewater region, North Carolina's rivers slow and widen as they spread across the Atlantic Coastal Plain. The pace of life in this rural area slows considerably as well. Extending about one hundred miles (161 km) inland, the Tidewater covers a great deal of marshland as well as the southern end of the Great Dismal Swamp. Because of their shallow estuaries, North Carolina's rivers don't make useful points of entry for shipping. However, the abundance of shrimp, blue crab, and flounder in the state's coastal waters makes them excellent for commercial fishing.

Overall, North Carolina ranks among the top ten states in industrial jobs. Yet wages remain low because so many of those jobs, especially in the tobacco industry, require little skill or training.

The thirteen thousand Cherokee in North Carolina make up one of the largest Native American populations east of the Mississippi River. Their reservation is located at the base of the Great Smoky Mountains, where their ancestors fled during the late 1830s to escape forced removal by the government.

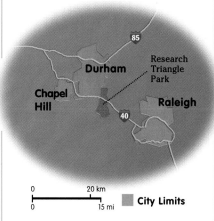

Since 1959, local business leaders have been working with the three Triangle universities—Duke (in Durham), North Carolina State (in Raleigh), and the University of North Carolina at Chapel Hill—to create a world-class research facility. The result, Research Triangle Park, specializes in such high-tech fields as supercomputing and biotechnology.

The long, thin islands that fringe much of North Carolina's coast are called the Outer Banks. These enormous sandbars protect the mainland from high winds and erosion caused by the pounding Atlantic surf.

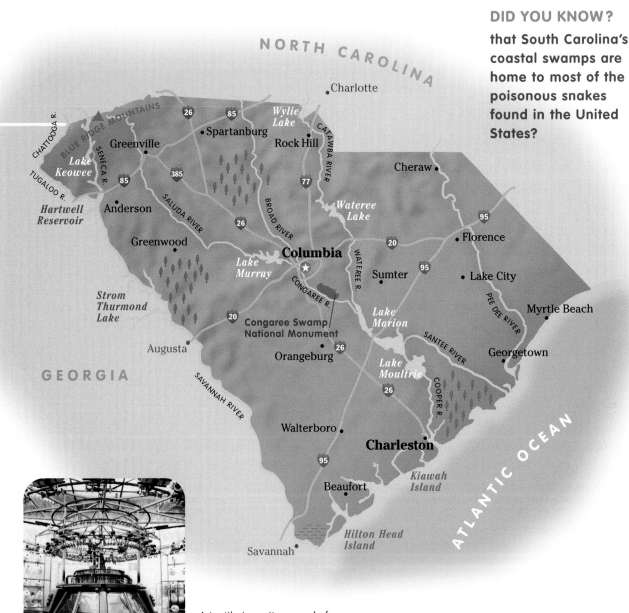

LEGEND

LEGEND

Interstate Highways	State Capital	National Parks and Refuges	National Forests	Marshlands	Highest Point	0 ——— miles ——— 50 / 0 ——— kilometers ——— 80

NORTH CAROLINA

DID YOU KNOW?

that South Carolina's coastal swamps are home to most of the poisonous snakes found in the United States?

Charlotte

BLUE RIDGE MOUNTAINS
CHATTOOGA R.
Wylie Lake
Spartanburg
Rock Hill
CATAWBA RIVER
Greenville
Lake Keowee
SENECA R.
TUGALOO R.
Hartwell Reservoir
Anderson
SALUDA RIVER
BROAD RIVER
Cheraw
Wateree Lake
Greenwood
Lake Murray
Columbia
Florence
WATEREE R.
Sumter
Lake City
Strom Thurmond Lake
CONGAREE R.
PEE DEE RIVER
Myrtle Beach
Augusta
Congaree Swamp National Monument
Orangeburg
Lake Marion
Georgetown
SANTEE RIVER
GEORGIA
SAVANNAH RIVER
Lake Moultrie
COOPER R.
Walterboro
Charleston
ATLANTIC OCEAN
Beaufort
Kiawah Island
Savannah
Hilton Head Island

A textile is an item made from woven or knitted cloth. In South Carolina's Textile Belt, which runs through Spartanburg and Greenville, owners of textile factories benefit from a relatively low cost of labor.

273 miles (439 km)

ABOUT SOUTH CAROLINA

NICKNAME: Palmetto State
CAPITAL: Columbia
STATEHOOD: May 23, 1788 (8th)
MOTTO: While I breathe, I hope.

POPULATION: 4,063,011 (26th)
AREA: 32,008 sq. mi. (40th)
(82,865 sq km)
HIGHEST POINT: 3,560 ft. (Sassafras Mt.)
LOWEST POINT: Sea level (Atlantic Ocean)

FLOWER: Yellow jessamine
TREE: Palmetto
BIRD: Carolina wren
FISH: Striped bass

South Carolina

South Carolina, like its neighbors, was once an agricultural state dependent on cotton and slave labor. Since the Civil War, however, tobacco and greenhouse plants have over-taken cotton as the most important crops, just as other sectors of the economy have overtaken agriculture. Yet South Carolina retains much of its pre–Civil War cultural heritage. For example, the state's tradition of soldiering has been preserved at both The Citadel in Charleston, one of the nation's premier military colleges, and the renowned Marine Corps training center on Parris Island, near Beaufort.

When it comes to geography, the people of South Carolina like to keep things simple: They call the flat land near the coast the Low Country and everything else the Up Country. Covering about two thirds of the state, the Low Country—what geographers call the Atlantic Coastal Plain—features many slow-moving rivers that feed swamps and marshes near the coast.

The Up Country—or, more formally, the Piedmont Plateau—begins just west of Columbia, the state capital. Rising gradually from east to west, the Piedmont ends at the Blue Ridge Mountains, which cut across the northwestern corner of the state. Columbia itself sits atop a line of sandy hills marking the point at which the South Carolina shoreline once stood millions of years ago.

Many black descendants of slaves live on the Sea Islands, extending south into Georgia and Florida. Isolation has helped preserve their unique language, Gullah, which mixes seventeenth-century English with several African languages. *Goober* (meaning "peanut") and *hoodoo* (meaning "bad luck") were both originally Gullah words.

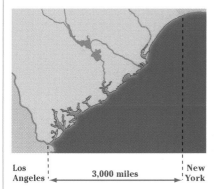

Los Angeles ←——— 3,000 miles ———→ New York

It's a Stretch
As the crow flies, South Carolina's coastline is 187 miles (301 km) long. However, because there are so many inlets and islands south of Georgetown, the coastline that you would walk along is actually much longer. If you could pull it straight, it would be about 3,000 miles (about 5,000 km) long—approximately the distance from Los Angeles to New York City.

From Pawleys Island (near Georgetown) to the North Carolina border stretches a sixty-mile (hundred-kilometer) crescent of white-sand beach called the Grand Strand. First among Grand Strand resorts is Myrtle Beach, a top-ten U.S. tourist destination.

Interstate
Highways

State
Capital

National
Parks and Refuges

National
Forests

▲
Highest Point

0   miles   50
0   kilometers   80

During World War II, the War Department built in a hidden Cumberland Mountain valley a top-secret town for scientists working on the atom bomb. Today, researchers at the Oak Ridge National Laboratory conduct all sorts of experiments, such as this one to help detect airborne pollutants.

An aerial view of Oak Ridge National Laboratory.

DID YOU KNOW?

that Tennessee's only large natural lake, Reelfoot, was created when violent earthquakes in 1811 and 1812 formed a depression into which water from the Mississippi River flowed?

430 miles (692 km)

ABOUT TENNESSEE

NICKNAME: Volunteer State

CAPITAL: Nashville

STATEHOOD: June 1, 1796 (16th)

MOTTO: Agriculture and commerce.

POPULATION: 5,740,021 (16th)

AREA: 42,146 sq. mi. (36th)
(109,111 sq km)

HIGHEST POINT: 6,643 ft. (Clingmans Dome)

LOWEST POINT: 178 ft. (Mississippi River)

FLOWER: Iris

TREE: Tulip tree

BIRD: Mockingbird

Tennessee

Tennessee has always been a divided state. During the Civil War, for example, the mountain people of eastern Tennessee remained loyal to the Union while the residents of middle and western Tennessee seceded to join the Confederacy. As a result, more Civil War battles were fought in Tennessee than in any other state except Virginia.

In many ways, Tennessee remains a divided state, caught between North and South. Its culture, especially in western Tennessee, is profoundly southern in style and taste. Tennessee's economy, however, is much more northern in character. Because 70 percent of the state's land is considered unfit for cultivation, Tennessee has industrialized more rapidly than its neighbors. Until recently, the chemical industry was ranked first in the state, but now, with new automobile factories in Spring Hill (Saturn) and Smyrna (Nissan), transportation equipment tops the list of its products.

Rugged eastern Tennessee takes in both the Great Smoky Mountains and the high, hilly Cumberland Plateau. West of the Cumberland Mountains sits the Nashville Basin, the most prominent geographical feature of middle Tennessee, which ends at the Tennessee River. The flatlands on the other side of that river make up western Tennessee, whose principal city is Memphis. In addition to being the second largest inland port on the Mississippi, Memphis is the birthplace of rock'n'roll music. From 1948, the city was home to Elvis Presley, whose Graceland mansion still receives 650,000 visitors a year.

Nashville, the Tennessee state capital, is probably better known as the Country Music Capital of the World. Ever since radio station WSM began broadcasting live performances from the Grand Ole Opry in 1925, songwriters and performers have flocked to Nashville's Music Row to make it in the music business.

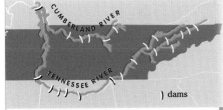

A Powerful River

In 1933, Congress created the Tennessee Valley Authority (TVA). Its mission was to build dams along the Tennessee River that would control flooding, improve navigation, and generate electricity. The TVA currently operates twenty-nine dams producing cheap hydroelectric power.

The Great Smoky Mountains of eastern Tennessee get their name from the bluish haze that usually covers them. This "smoke" is actually a mixture of water vapor and evaporated plant oils.

57

LEGEND

 20 Interstate Highways

⊛ State Capital

■ National Parks and Refuges

▦ Marshlands

▲ Highest Point

| 0 | miles | 50 |
| 0 | kilometers | 80 |

The hub of the navy's Atlantic fleet is Hampton Roads, the deepwater channel through which the James River flows into Chesapeake Bay. Norfolk, site of the world's largest naval base, serves as home port to sixty-six ships, while Newport News Shipbuilding, the largest privately owned U.S. shipyard, builds everything from tugboats to nuclear-powered aircraft carriers.

MARYLAND

Baltimore

Winchester

Shenandoah National Park

81

Arlington • Washington, D.C.

66 Alexandria

WEST VIRGINIA

Harrisonburg

Staunton

Fredericksburg

Charlottesville

SHENANDOAH R.

POTOMAC R.

RAPPAHANNOCK R.

Chesapeake Bay

95

64

64 Lexington

JAMES RIVER

Richmond ★

YORK R.

KY.

77

Roanoke

ALLEGHENY MOUNTAINS

Lynchburg

• Appomattox

Petersburg

64 Williamsburg

ATLANTIC OCEAN

Pulaski

81

BLUE RIDGE MOUNTAINS

ROANOKE RIVER

85

Newport News

Hampton

Wytheville

NEW RIVER

Buggs Island Lake

95 Norfolk

Virginia Beach

CLINCH RIVER

81

77

Bristol

Danville

Lake Gaston

Chesapeake

Great Dismal Swamp National Wildlife Refuge

Johnson City

TN.

NORTH CAROLINA

• Raleigh

DID YOU KNOW?

that the Pentagon in Arlington, with 23,000 workers and 284 rest rooms, is one of the world's largest office buildings?

◀———— 440 miles (708 km) ————▶

ABOUT VIRGINIA

NICKNAME: Old Dominion

CAPITAL: Richmond

STATEHOOD: June 25, 1788 (10th)

MOTTO: Thus always to tyrants.

POPULATION: 7,187,734 (12th)

AREA: 42,777 sq. mi. (35th)
(110,745 sq km)

HIGHEST POINT: 5,729 ft. (Mount Rogers)

LOWEST POINT: Sea level (Atlantic Ocean)

FLOWER: Flowering dogwood

TREE: Flowering dogwood

BIRD: Cardinal

Virginia

In George Washington's time, Virginia was a rich agricultural state. Today, however, farming is primarily confined to small family operations. The biggest employer now is the federal government, which accounts for nearly one fourth of the state's total income. The Hampton Roads naval base alone generates some seven billion dollars a year.

The people who live in Virginia's northern counties, many of whom commute to jobs in Washington, D.C., reflect the multicultural makeup of the nation's capital. On the other hand, Richmond still adheres to a recognizably southern way of life. In this regard, the former Confederate stronghold now forms a convenient bridge between North and South.

Like other southern seaboard states, Virginia slopes down from mountains in the west to marshland in the east. The most important ranges in Virginia, the Blue Ridge and Allegheny mountains, belong to the Appalachian chain. Below them lie the rolling hills of the Piedmont, which gradually descend to the fall line. Here the land "falls" abruptly to the Atlantic Coastal Plain, creating river rapids and waterfalls. (Many Virginia cities—including Alexandria, Fredericksburg, Richmond, and Petersburg—grew up along the fall line to take advantage of its cheap waterpower.) Finally, the low sandy plain surrounding Chesapeake Bay is called the Tidewater because of the effect that the ocean tides have on its inlets and waterways.

Virginia boasts an unusually large number of historic sites, from the homes of George Washington and Thomas Jefferson to important Revolutionary and Civil War battlefields. Among the most popular sites is Colonial Williamsburg, a restoration designed to show visitors the colonial capital as Washington and Jefferson knew it.

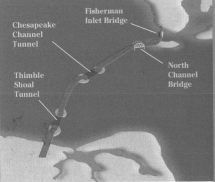

The twenty-three-mile-long (thirty-seven-kilometer-long) Chesapeake Bay Bridge-Tunnel connects the southern side of Hampton Roads with Virginia's Eastern Shore. The structure, the longest of its kind in the world, includes two bridges, four artificial islands, and a pair of tunnels that pass under the bay's two main shipping channels.

The scenic, fertile Shenandoah Valley lies between the Blue Ridge and Allegheny mountains. Its name, of Native American origin, means "daughter of the stars."

Interstate Highways

State Capital

National Parks and Refuges

National Forests

Highest Point

| 0 | miles | 50 |
| 0 | kilometers | 80 |

DID YOU KNOW?

that in West Virginia's thin northern panhandle the city of Weirton stretches across the entire state?

Pittsburgh

Weirton

PENNSYLVANIA

Wheeling

70

79

OHIO

Morgantown

68

MD.

Cumberland

Hagerstown

Harpers Ferry National Historical Park

Fairmont

Clarksburg

OHIO RIVER

NORTH BRANCH POTOMAC R.

Keyser

POTOMAC R.

Martinsburg

Parkersburg

SOUTH BRANCH POTOMAC R.

81

SHENANDOAH R.

Buckhannon

77

79

Elkins

KANAWHA R.

Sutton Lake

ALLEGHENY MOUNTAINS

VIRGINIA

OHIO RIVER

64

Charleston

ELK RIVER

BIG SANDY RIVER

Huntington

South Charleston

GAULEY RIVER

Spruce Knob Seneca Rocks National Reservation Area

Charlottesville

GUYANDOTTE RIVER

77

64

Oak Hill

Beckley

NEW RIVER

64

KENTUCKY

TUG FORK RIVER

77

Bluefield

Roanoke

Since the nineteenth century, the health of West Virginia's economy has depended on coal mining. The huge seams of soft bituminous coal that underlie the state have made it the nation's second largest coal producer (behind Wyoming). Yet this dependence has also bound generations of West Virginians to hard, dangerous work in the mines.

265 miles (426 km)

ABOUT WEST VIRGINIA

NICKNAME: Mountain State

CAPITAL: Charleston

STATEHOOD: June 20, 1863 (35th)

MOTTO: Mountaineers are always free.

POPULATION: 1,801,916 (37th)

AREA: 24,231 sq. mi. (41st) (62,731 sq km)

HIGHEST POINT: 4,861 ft. (Spruce Knob)

LOWEST POINT: 240 ft. (Potomac River)

FLOWER: Rhododendron

TREE: Sugar maple

BIRD: Cardinal

FISH: Brook trout

West Virginia

Few states are as rugged as West Virginia. Except for a handful of floodplains surrounding its major rivers, there's almost no level ground. This makes farming difficult and frustrates all sorts of economic development because moving things around is so hard. As a result, West Virginia has remained a state of small, isolated communities tucked away in steep, narrow hollows. Only one in every three West Virginians lives in a city.

On the other hand, the mountains do supply West Virginia with the mineral wealth that is its main source of income. In addition to coal, West Virginians mine silica-rich sandstone for glassware (and most U.S. marbles), clay for pottery, and salt for dyes, paints, and plastics. The Native American word *kanawha*, meaning "place of the white stone," refers to the large deposits of salt in the Kanawha and Ohio river valleys.

Passing approximately through Elkins, the Allegheny Front separates the Allegheny Plateau, which covers the western two thirds of the state, from the Appalachian Ridge and Valley system in the east. Millions of years ago, the Allegheny Plateau was a high flatland, but over time rivers have eroded the softer rock, creating the present maze of hills and valleys.

Like most natives of Appalachia, West Virginians take great pride in their folk culture, especially the "mountain music" they play on fiddles, dulcimers, mandolins, and other homemade string instruments. Nationally syndicated *Mountain Stage*, produced by West Virginia Public Radio, features this music along with contemporary folk, blues, and even rock 'n' roll.

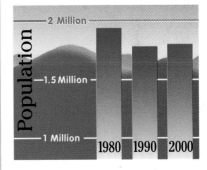

During the 1980s, West Virginia lost more population than any other state, falling from 1,950,186 residents in 1980 to 1,793,477 in 1990. Most of those who left were young people from rural areas who were having trouble finding jobs. Since 1992, the population has stabilized at about 1,800,000.

All of West Virginia lies within the Appalachian Mountains. The state's highest point is Spruce Knob, from whose summit this view was taken.

CANADA

LAKE SUPERIOR

LAKE HURON

Minnesota
page 72

Wisconsin
page 78

LAKE MICHIGAN

Michigan
page 70

LAKE ERIE

MISSOURI RIVER

Iowa
page 68

ILLINOIS RIVER

WABASH RIVER

Ohio
page 76

Illinois
page 64

Indiana
page 66

OHIO RIVER

Missouri
page 74

MISSISSIPPI RIVER

Midwest

During the last Ice Age, huge glaciers covered nearly all the Midwest. Like unfrozen water, these glaciers also flowed, if very slowly. Their movement had the same effect as a giant bulldozer, flattening the land and leaving behind a thick layer of mixed clay and stone, called till. Most of this region now belongs to what geographers call the Dissected Till Plains. (*Dissected* means "cut up," referring in this case to the way that rivers and streams have cut up the tableland.)

20 Interstate Highways

 ✪ State Capital

🌲🌲🌲 National Forests

▲ Highest Point

| 0 | miles | 50 |
| 0 | kilometers | 80 |

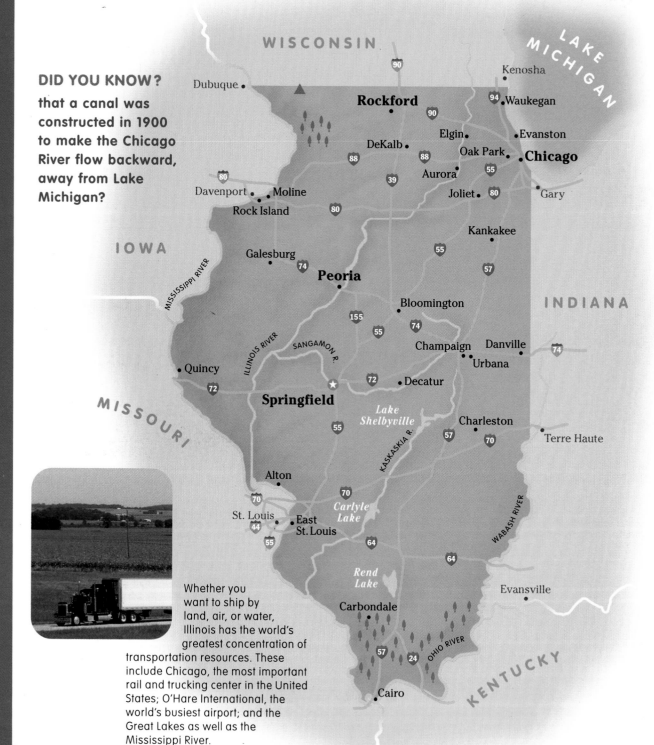

DID YOU KNOW? that a canal was constructed in 1900 to make the Chicago River flow backward, away from Lake Michigan?

WISCONSIN

LAKE MICHIGAN

Dubuque

Kenosha

Rockford

Waukegan

Elgin
Evanston

DeKalb
Oak Park
Chicago

Aurora

Davenport
Moline
Joliet
Gary

Rock Island

IOWA

MISSISSIPPI RIVER

Galesburg

Kankakee

Peoria

INDIANA

ILLINOIS RIVER

Bloomington

SANGAMON R.

Champaign
Danville

Quincy

Urbana

Decatur

Springfield

Lake Shelbyville

Charleston

Terre Haute

MISSOURI

KASKASKIA R.

Alton

Carlyle Lake

St. Louis
East St. Louis

WABASH RIVER

Rend Lake

Evansville

Carbondale

OHIO RIVER

Cairo

KENTUCKY

Whether you want to ship by land, air, or water, Illinois has the world's greatest concentration of transportation resources. These include Chicago, the most important rail and trucking center in the United States; O'Hare International, the world's busiest airport; and the Great Lakes as well as the Mississippi River.

◄—————— 211 miles (339 km) ——————►

ABOUT ILLINOIS

NICKNAME: Prairie State

CAPITAL: Springfield

STATEHOOD: December 3, 1818 (21st)

MOTTO: State sovereignty— national union.

POPULATION: 12,482,301 (5th)

AREA: 57,918 sq. mi. (25th) (149,943 sq km)

HIGHEST POINT: 1,235 ft. (Charles Mound)

LOWEST POINT: 279 ft. (Mississippi River)

FLOWER: Native violet

TREE: White oak

BIRD: Cardinal

FISH: Bluegill

Illinois

If you live in Illinois, you're either a Chicagoan or a downstater. Being a Chicagoan means that you live in the nation's third largest city or one of its many suburbs. Everyone else is a downstater. Because Chicagoans significantly outnumber downstaters in Illinois, they tend to monopolize state politics. Downstaters sometimes joke that Chicagoans believe their immediate neighbors are New York City and Los Angeles. Nevertheless, all Illinoisans take great pride in the fact that Abraham Lincoln spent his entire adult life in the state. (Interestingly, Lincoln lived in New Salem and later in Springfield, but never in Chicago.)

Overall, Chicago has benefited greatly from its central location and easy access to both the Great Lakes and the Mississippi River. Because the city is a major transportation hub, it can easily import raw materials and then ship out finished goods. This has helped it become a major U.S. manufacturing center, second only to the Los Angeles area in the number of manufacturing jobs it offers.

Unlike industrial Chicago, downstate Illinois is rural and agricultural. Primarily flat, with hilly areas only in the northwest and south, it lies almost entirely within the Dissected Till Plains, whose flat topography and rich glacial soil present ideal conditions for farming. As elsewhere in the midwestern farm belt, the major crops in Illinois are corn and soybeans.

Although blues originated among African Americans in the rural South about 1900, the music quickly migrated north along with southern blacks seeking industrial jobs. During the Great Depression, Big Bill Broonzy and Sonny Boy Williamson became popular performers in Chicago. After World War II, Muddy Waters, Elmore James, and Howlin' Wolf (pictured here) made Chicago-style urban blues world famous.

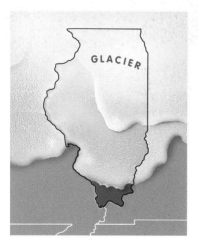

During the last Ice Age, glaciers covered nearly all of Illinois. These huge masses of ice flattened the state, grinding down hills and leaving behind a layer of mineral-rich soil. In other words, they turned Illinois into excellent farmland.

The skyscraper, first developed in Chicago, continues to dominate that city's skyline. Until the 1997 completion of the 1,483-foot (452-meter) Petronas Towers in Malaysia, the 1,450-foot (442-meter) Sears Tower was the world's tallest building.

Interstate Highways

State Capital

National Parks and Refuges

National Forests

Highest Point

0   miles   50
0   kilometers   80

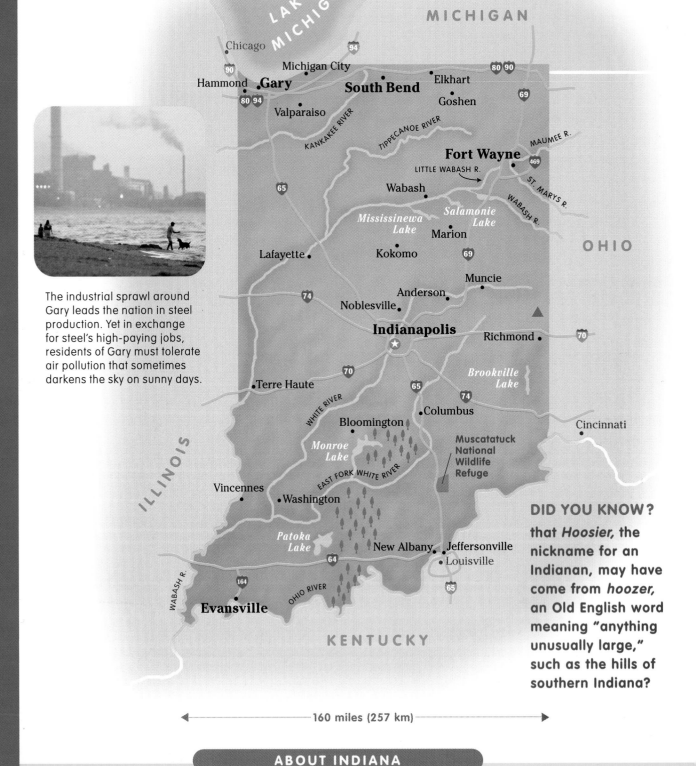

LAKE MICHIGAN

MICHIGAN

Chicago

94

Michigan City

90

Hammond   **Gary**

South Bend

Elkhart

80 90

80 94

Valparaiso

Goshen

69

KANKAKEE RIVER

TIPPECANOE RIVER

MAUMEE R.

Fort Wayne

469

LITTLE WABASH R.

ST. MARYS R.

65

Wabash

WABASH R.

Mississinewa Lake

Salamonie Lake

OHIO

Marion

Lafayette

Kokomo

69

Muncie

74

Anderson

Noblesville

Indianapolis

Richmond

70

70

Brookville Lake

65

Terre Haute

74

Columbus

Cincinnati

WHITE RIVER

Bloomington

Monroe Lake

Muscatatuck National Wildlife Refuge

ILLINOIS

EAST FORK WHITE RIVER

Vincennes

Washington

Patoka Lake

New Albany

Jeffersonville

Louisville

WABASH R.

164

64

OHIO RIVER

65

Evansville

KENTUCKY

The industrial sprawl around Gary leads the nation in steel production. Yet in exchange for steel's high-paying jobs, residents of Gary must tolerate air pollution that sometimes darkens the sky on sunny days.

DID YOU KNOW?

that *Hoosier,* the nickname for an Indianan, may have come from *hoozer,* an Old English word meaning "anything unusually large," such as the hills of southern Indiana?

◄———— 160 miles (257 km) ————►

ABOUT INDIANA

NICKNAME: Hoosier State

CAPITAL: Indianapolis

STATEHOOD: December 11, 1816 (19th)

MOTTO: The crossroads of America.

POPULATION: 6,114,745 (14th)

AREA: 36,420 sq. mi. (38th)
(94,287 sq km)

HIGHEST POINT: 1,257 ft. (Franklin Township)

LOWEST POINT: 320 ft. (Ohio River)

FLOWER: Peony

TREE: Tulip tree

BIRD: Cardinal

Indiana

The landscape of Indiana, like that of Illinois and Iowa, was shaped by the glaciers that covered the Midwest during the last Ice Age. In the northern third of the state, these glaciers left behind many hollows that became kettle lakes. In central Indiana, they flattened the land and deposited a rocky debris called till. Over time, the sand, clay, and minerals that made up the till eroded into a thick layer of highly fertile soil. Only the southern sixth of Indiana, a region rich in coal and limestone, escaped the glaciers, and so only its hills were preserved.

Farms established on Indiana's central flatlands flourished during the nineteenth century. Since 1900, however, manufacturing has become increasingly important to the state, particularly in its northwestern corner, which abuts Lake Michigan. Gary, for example, became a popular location for steel plants because it lay halfway between the iron ranges of Minnesota and the coalfields of southern Indiana.

The population of Indiana is only 8 percent black. Yet the city of Gary is 84 percent black because nearly all the blacks in Indiana live there—or in Fort Wayne or Indianapolis. The rest of the state, except for a large Polish community in South Bend, is typically white, Protestant, and English, Irish, or German in descent.

No sport arouses the passion of Hoosiers the way that basketball does. That's why the state's annual high school basketball tournament is called Hoosier Hysteria. Perhaps basketball, a winter sport, is especially popular in Indiana, a farming state, because it doesn't have to compete with spring planting or the fall harvest season.

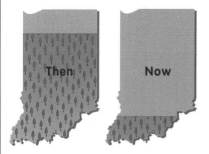

Where Have All the Forests Gone?
When white settlers first came to Indiana during the early nineteenth century, about 80 percent of the state was covered with trees, especially beeches, sycamores, oaks, and maples. Then these pioneers began clearing the land for farms. Today, only 16 percent of Indiana remains forested.

Indiana limestone has been used to face the Empire State Building, the Pentagon, and many other celebrated structures. Workers in the quarries around Bloomington, which produce the finest limestone, are called cutters.

🛣 20	⚙	⬛	🔺	0 miles 50	
Interstate Highways	State Capital	National Parks and Refuges	Highest Point	0 kilometers 80	

DID YOU KNOW?

that nearly nine out of ten Iowans graduate from high school (compared to seven out of ten nationwide)?

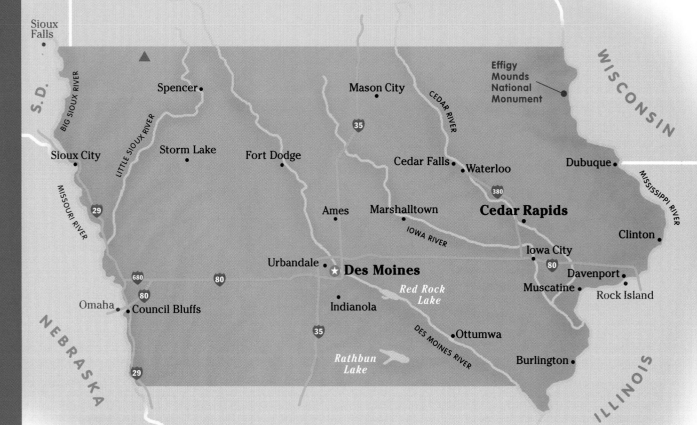

MINNESOTA

WISCONSIN

S.D.

Sioux Falls

🔺

Spencer

Mason City

Effigy Mounds National Monument

CEDAR RIVER

BIG SIOUX RIVER

LITTLE SIOUX RIVER

Sioux City

Storm Lake

Fort Dodge

35

Cedar Falls

Waterloo

Dubuque

MISSISSIPPI RIVER

MISSOURI RIVER

29

Ames

Marshalltown

Cedar Rapids

380

IOWA RIVER

Clinton

Urbandale

680

80

⭐ **Des Moines**

Red Rock Lake

Iowa City

80

Davenport

Muscatine

Rock Island

NEBRASKA

80

Omaha

Council Bluffs

Indianola

35

Ottumwa

DES MOINES RIVER

Burlington

ILLINOIS

29

Rathbun Lake

MISSOURI

Most Iowans work in jobs related to farming. Although just 4 percent actually farm the land, many more have jobs in food-processing plants or factories making farm equipment. Waterloo has meat-packing and tractor plants, Cedar Rapids and Keokuk have large cereal mills, and Sioux City has the world's largest popcorn factory (pictured here).

◄———————— 324 miles (521 km) ————————►

ABOUT IOWA

NICKNAME: Hawkeye State

CAPITAL: Des Moines

STATEHOOD: December 28, 1846 (29th)

MOTTO: Our liberties we prize and our rights we will maintain.

POPULATION: 2,923,179 (30th)

AREA: 56,276 sq. mi. (26th) (145,692 sq km)

HIGHEST POINT: 1,670 ft. (Ocheyedan Mound)

LOWEST POINT: 480 ft. (Mississippi River)

FLOWER: Wild rose

TREE: Oak

BIRD: Eastern goldfinch

Iowa

IOWA

Iowa's greatest resource is its fertile soil. Like that in the rest of the midwestern farm belt, Iowa's soil was deposited by glaciers that once covered the entire state. Now farms cover 92 percent of the land, producing one fifth of the nation's corn and also a fifth of its hogs.

Following a national trend, farms in Iowa have been increasing in size while decreasing in number. The cause of this has been large agricultural corporations buying up and merging small family spreads. In 1955, there were 193,000 farms in Iowa; today, there are merely half that number. Many small farmers, unable to compete, have gone bankrupt, threatening Iowa's small-town way of life. One way that the state has sought to stabilize its economy during bad farm cycles has been to encourage nonfarm industries, such as computer manufacturing in Cedar Rapids and insurance in Des Moines.

Most people think of Iowa as pancake flat, and central Iowa certainly is, but other parts of the state are hilly. In the northeastern corner, for instance, streams have eroded the bedrock to form rugged valleys. In fact, some of the bluffs lining the Mississippi River are four hundred feet (120 m) high. In the west, however, the hills bordering the Missouri River Valley are not uneroded bedrock but accumulations of windblown silt called loess.

Because Iowa is a state of small towns, it can't support the same cultural institutions, such as symphonies and museums, that states with large cities can. Instead, cultural life in Iowa is often centered on colleges and universities, such as the University of Iowa, which runs the prestigious Iowa Writers' Workshop.

The Uniform State
Because Iowa has an evenly distributed population and very few minorities (only 6 percent of the population), social scientists often use it as an example of "large-scale uniformity." This means that, compared to other states, Iowans are very much alike.

Each of Iowa's small towns is often little more than a few houses, some grain elevators, and a church. Most Iowans say they prefer life on that scale. Yet more and more have been forced by farm failures to take jobs in the cities.

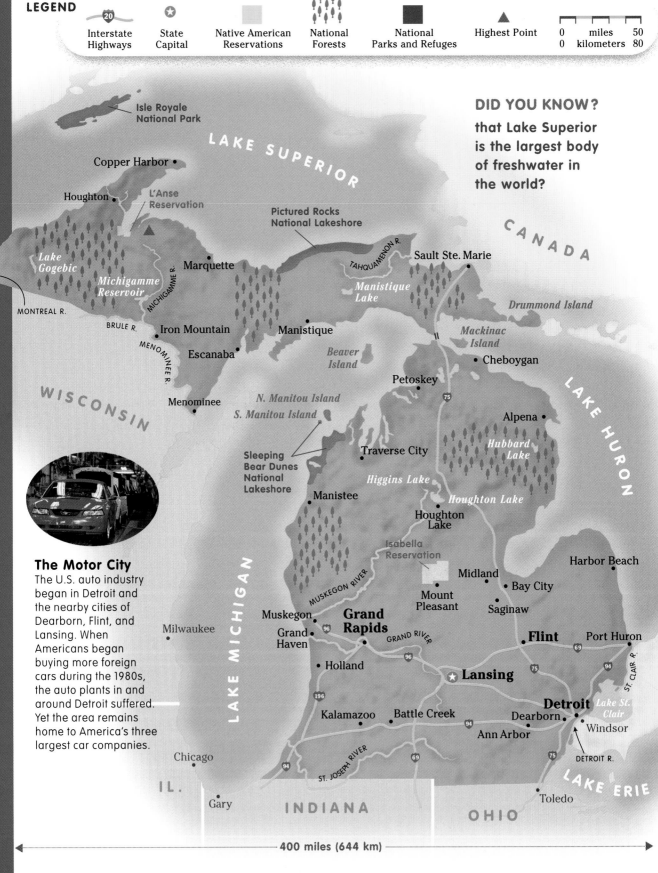

LEGEND

Interstate Highways | State Capital | Native American Reservations | National Forests | National Parks and Refuges | Highest Point

0 miles 50
0 kilometers 80

DID YOU KNOW?

that Lake Superior is the largest body of freshwater in the world?

Isle Royale National Park

LAKE SUPERIOR

Copper Harbor •

Houghton •   L'Anse Reservation

CANADA

Pictured Rocks National Lakeshore

Lake Gogebic

Michigamme Reservoir

MONTREAL R.

BRULE R.

MENOMINEE R.

MICHIGAMME R.

Marquette

Iron Mountain

Escanaba

Menominee

WISCONSIN

TAHQUAMENON R.

Sault Ste. Marie

Drummond Island

Manistique Lake

Manistique

Mackinac Island

Beaver Island

Cheboygan

Petoskey

N. Manitou Island
S. Manitou Island

Sleeping Bear Dunes National Lakeshore

Traverse City

Alpena •

LAKE HURON

Hubbard Lake

Higgins Lake

Houghton Lake

Houghton Lake

Manistee

Isabella Reservation

MUSKEGON RIVER

Mount Pleasant

Midland

Bay City

Harbor Beach

Saginaw

LAKE MICHIGAN

Muskegon

Grand Haven

Grand Rapids

GRAND RIVER

Flint

Port Huron

Milwaukee •

Holland

Lansing

Detroit

Lake St. Clair

ST. CLAIR R.

Kalamazoo

Battle Creek

Dearborn

Ann Arbor

Windsor

DETROIT R.

Chicago •

ST. JOSEPH RIVER

IL.

Gary •

INDIANA

OHIO

Toledo •

LAKE ERIE

⟵ 400 miles (644 km) ⟶

The Motor City

The U.S. auto industry began in Detroit and the nearby cities of Dearborn, Flint, and Lansing. When Americans began buying more foreign cars during the 1980s, the auto plants in and around Detroit suffered. Yet the area remains home to America's three largest car companies.

ABOUT MICHIGAN

NICKNAME: Wolverine State
CAPITAL: Lansing
STATEHOOD: January 26, 1837 (26th)
MOTTO: If you seek a beautiful peninsula, look around you.

POPULATION: 9,990,817 (8th)
AREA: 96,705 sq. mi. (11th) (250,358 sq km)
HIGHEST POINT: 1,979 ft. (Mount Arvon)
LOWEST POINT: 571 ft. (Lake Erie)

FLOWER: Apple blossom
TREE: White pine
BIRD: Robin
FISH: Brook trout

Michigan

A peninsula is a spit of land, shaped like a tongue, bounded on three sides by water. The state of Michigan is actually a pair of peninsulas, one divided from the other by the Straits of Mackinac (pronounced MACK-i-naw). Michigan's sometimes hilly, sometimes swampy Upper Peninsula is connected to the flatter, mitten-shaped Lower Peninsula by the Mackinac Bridge.

Michigan is called the Great Lakes State because it borders four of the five Great Lakes. As a result, shipping has always been an important business there. The locks at Sault Ste. Marie (nicknamed "the Soo") were opened in 1855 to service ships carrying timber and iron ore from Minnesota and the Upper Peninsula. These locks, which equalize the water level between Lake Superior and Lake Huron, are still among the world's busiest.

Michiganders in great numbers also use the Great Lakes for recreation. The rural Upper Peninsula doesn't have many people, but most of them fish. So do the carloads of Detroiters and Chicagoans who visit the Upper Peninsula each summer for a vacation out-of-doors. Despite the fact that it contains every one of Michigan's major cities and important industrial centers, the Lower Peninsula is no less outdoorsy. In fact, Michiganders of both peninsulas own more boats than residents of any other state.

The fish boil has been a Great Lakes tradition since the nineteenth century. It was devised by Scandinavian immigrants who wanted an easy way to cook whitefish and lake trout. For a traditional outdoor fish boil, Michiganders cook chunks of fish, potatoes, and onions in seasoned water over large wood fires.

Michigan's Slice of the Pie
Michigan produces about 75 percent of the sour pie cherries grown in the United States. The area around Traverse City is particularly good for growing cherries because Lake Michigan moderates the weather there, tempering the frosts and cooling the orchards during summer.

Large ships haul cargo from the Midwest to the East (and beyond) using the St. Lawrence Seaway. This system of canals, locks, and dams joins the Great Lakes to the Atlantic Ocean.

20 Interstate Highways

State Capital

Native American Reservations

National Forests

National Parks and Refuges

Marshlands

▲ Highest Point

0	miles	50
0	kilometers	80

The Mesabi Range once produced more than half the world's iron ore. The richest deposits have long been depleted, but the area around Hibbing still fills about two thirds of the U.S. need with a plentiful low-grade ore called taconite. Mining companies get at the taconite by stripping away the thin soil and digging large open pits.

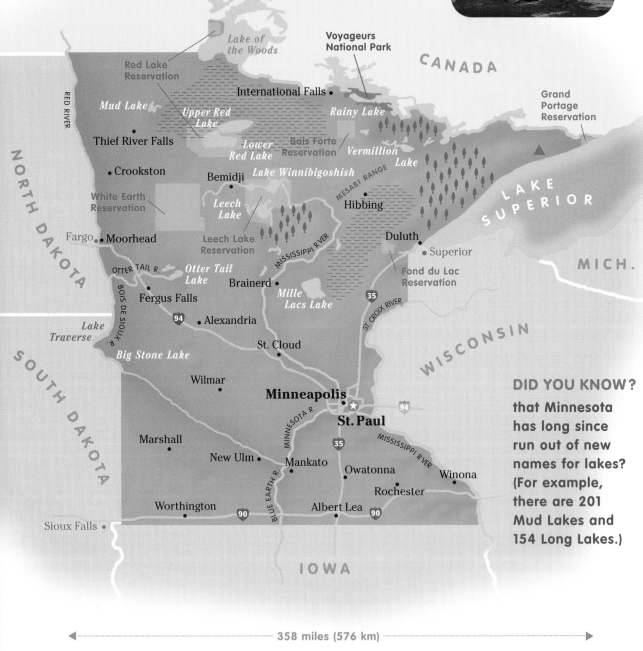

Lake of the Woods

Voyageurs National Park

CANADA

Red Lake Reservation

International Falls

Rainy Lake

Grand Portage Reservation

RED RIVER

Mud Lake

Upper Red Lake

Thief River Falls

Lower Red Lake

Bois Forte Reservation

Vermillion Lake

Crookston

Bemidji

Lake Winnibigoshish

MESABI RANGE

LAKE SUPERIOR

White Earth Reservation

Leech Lake

Hibbing

MISSISSIPPI RIVER

Duluth

MICH.

Fargo • Moorhead

Leech Lake Reservation

Superior

Fond du Lac Reservation

OTTER TAIL R.

Otter Tail Lake

Brainerd

35

BOIS DE SIOUX R.

Fergus Falls

Mille Lacs Lake

ST. CROIX RIVER

Lake Traverse

94

Alexandria

St. Cloud

WISCONSIN

Big Stone Lake

Wilmar

Minneapolis

94

St. Paul

MINNESOTA R.

Marshall

35

MISSISSIPPI RIVER

New Ulm

Mankato

Owatonna

Winona

BLUE EARTH R.

Rochester

Worthington

90

Albert Lea

90

Sioux Falls •

NORTH DAKOTA

SOUTH DAKOTA

IOWA

DID YOU KNOW?

that Minnesota has long since run out of new names for lakes? (For example, there are 201 Mud Lakes and 154 Long Lakes.)

← 358 miles (576 km) →

ABOUT MINNESOTA

NICKNAME: Gopher State
CAPITAL: St. Paul
STATEHOOD: May 11, 1858 (32nd)
MOTTO: Star of the North.

POPULATION: 4,972,294 (21st)
AREA: 86,943 sq. mi. (12th)
(225,085 sq km)
HIGHEST POINT: 2,301 ft. (Eagle Mountain)
LOWEST POINT: 600 ft. (Lake Superior)

FLOWER: Pink and white lady's slipper
TREE: Norway pine
BIRD: Common loon
FISH: Walleye

Minnesota

More than half of Minnesota's population lives in or near the Twin Cities of Minneapolis and St. Paul, built along the Mississippi River at the head of its navigable waters. Indeed, the Twin Cities are the largest metropolitan area for hundreds of miles around. As a result, they've become an important transportation, business, and cultural center for the entire upper Midwest.

Minneapolis and St. Paul are such cosmopolitan cities that a minority presence there doesn't seem unusual, yet that isn't the case elsewhere in Minnesota. Overwhelmingly, Minnesota's residents are white, mostly of German and Scandinavian descent, accounting for 93 percent of the population statewide. Even in a city such as Duluth, all the minorities taken together account for just 4 percent of the population.

Minnesota calls itself the Land of Ten Thousand Lakes, even though there are more than fifteen thousand of them. Most were left behind when the midwestern glaciers receded after the last Ice Age. In the Mesabi Range, those glaciers bulldozed away rock covering large iron ore deposits. Elsewhere, they dumped the same rich soil that makes Iowa farmland so fertile. Not surprisingly, mining and dairying have both become important industries in the state. Minnesota's dairy cows rank among the national leaders in butter production, while Duluth remains one of the world's busiest freshwater ports, largely because of iron ore and grain shipments.

What most Americans know about Minnesota, true or not, they probably learned from Garrison Keillor, host of *A Prairie Home Companion*. Keillor's weekly radio variety show, broadcast live from St. Paul, features "The News from Lake Wobegon," an account of recent events in Keillor's imaginary hometown "where all the children are above average."

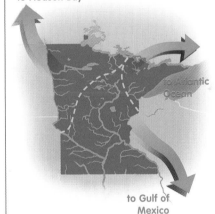

to Hudson Bay

to Gulf of Mexico

Minnesota straddles three continental watersheds. Southern Minnesota drains into the Mississippi River (and thereby the Gulf of Mexico). In the west, the Red River flows north toward Canada's Hudson Bay. In the northeast, the region around Duluth drains into the Atlantic Ocean via Lake Superior.

Canoeing is particularly popular in Minnesota, especially along the upper Mississippi River. The source of the Mississippi can be found at Lake Itasca, near Bemidji.

Interstate Highways | State Capital | National Parks and Refuges | National Forests | Highest Point

| 0 | miles | 50 |
| 0 | kilometers | 80 |

Among the most important of Missouri's diverse industries is the manufacture of transportation equipment. Missourians make automobiles, limousines, railroad cars, aircraft, and even spacecraft. Workers at the factory pictured here assemble fire engines.

IOWA

Squaw Creek National Wildlife Refuge

NEB.

DES MOINES R.

Maryville

Kirksville

Springfield

ILLINOIS

St. Joseph

GRAND RIVER

CHARITON RIVER

Hannibal

MISSOURI RIVER

Mark Twain Lake

Topeka

Independence

Kansas City

Columbia

St. Charles

Sedalia

MISSOURI RIVER

Jefferson City ☆

Washington

St. Louis

KANSAS

Harry S. Truman Reservoir

Lake of the Ozarks

OSAGE RIVER

MISSISSIPPI RIVER

Nevada

Stockton Lake

Rolla

Farmington

CURRENT RIVER

Cape Girardeau

Cairo

Springfield

ST. FRANCIS RIVER

Joplin

OZARK MTS.

Big Spring

West Plains

OKLAHOMA

Table Rock Lake

Branson

Bull Shoals Lake

Poplar Bluff

KY.

WHITE RIVER

ARKANSAS

TENN.

DID YOU KNOW?

that the town of Washington is the world's leading manufacturer of corncob pipes?

◄-------- 284 miles (457 km) --------►

ABOUT MISSOURI

NICKNAME: Show Me State
CAPITAL: Jefferson City
STATEHOOD: August 10, 1821 (24th)
MOTTO: Let the welfare of the people be the supreme law.

POPULATION: 5,629,707 (17th)
AREA: 69,709 sq. mi. (21st) (180,468 sq km)
HIGHEST POINT: 1,772 ft. (Taum Sauk Mt.)
LOWEST POINT: 230 ft. (St. Francis River)

FLOWER: Hawthorn
TREE: Flowering dogwood
BIRD: Bluebird

Missouri

From any map it's easy to tell that the path of the Missouri River determined settlement patterns in the state: St. Louis, for example, was founded near the point at which the Missouri flows into the Mississippi, while Kansas City was built at the junction of the Missouri and Kansas rivers.

River transportation, once the state's most important business, has declined since the end of the nineteenth century, yet St. Louis has remained a national crossroads and midwestern cultural center, home to academically superior Washington University as well as a nationally respected symphony orchestra and art museum. Although the Catholic church in St. Louis isn't as vital as it once was, the city remains important enough to American Catholicism that it received a rare papal visit in 1999.

Topographically, Missouri is the most diverse state in the Midwest. The Missouri River marks the southernmost reach of the glaciers that once covered the region. (In fact, the Missouri's channel was carved by glacial meltwater running southeast into the Mississippi.) The land north of the Missouri, with its flattened contours and fertile glacial soil, belongs to the Corn Belt. South of the Missouri rise the forested hills and low mountains of the Ozark Plateau. In western Missouri, the prairies of the Great Plains begin, while in the southeastern corner of the state, in an area called the Bootheel, farmers till the rich bottom-lands of the Mississippi floodplain.

Show Me
In 1899, Missouri congressman Willard D. Vandiver told an audience in Philadelphia, "I'm from Missouri. You've got to show me." That attitude of intelligent skepticism was later raised to a mythic level by Independence native Harry Truman, who as president kept on his White House desk a famous sign that read, I'M FROM MISSOURI.

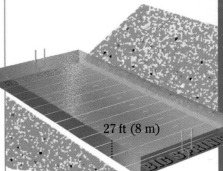

27 ft (8 m)

Quite a Big Spring
Underground rivers in the Ozarks have, over time, eaten away large sections of the limestone bedrock, creating some of the biggest springs in the world. Big Spring, the nation's largest, pumps about 11.5 million gallons (43.5 million l) of water into the Current River each hour. That's enough flow to cover a football field with a column of water twenty-seven feet deep.

The 630-foot-tall (192-meter-tall) Gateway Arch celebrates St. Louis's role as the primary nineteenth-century transportation link between the East and the West. Today, St. Louis remains a key trucking and shipping center.

LEGEND

20 Interstate Highways	⭐ State Capital	⬛ National Parks and Refuges	🌲 National Forests	🔺 Highest Point	0 — miles — 50 0 — kilometers — 80

Every summer, Akron hosts the All-American Soap Box Derby. For more than a century, Akron led the world in tire research and production. Then foreign competitors caught up, and people began buying tires made elsewhere. Akron's city leaders are now searching for another industry to take rubber's place.

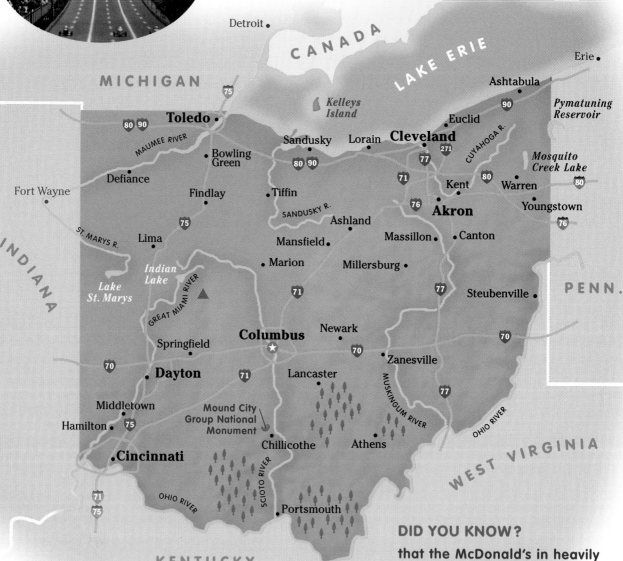

210 miles (338 km)

DID YOU KNOW?

that the McDonald's in heavily Amish Millersburg has a drive-through window at buggy height?

ABOUT OHIO

NICKNAME: Buckeye State

CAPITAL: Columbus

STATEHOOD: March 1, 1803 (17th)

MOTTO: With God, all things are possible.

POPULATION: 11,373,541 (7th)

AREA: 44,828 sq. mi. (34th)
(116,054 sq km)

HIGHEST POINT: 1,549 ft. (Campbell Hill)

LOWEST POINT: 455 ft. (Ohio River)

FLOWER: Scarlet carnation

TREE: Buckeye

BIRD: Cardinal

Ohio

Ohio is easy to cross, which is why most nineteenth-century pioneers passed through it on their journeys west. The state contains no natural barriers, such as deserts or mountain ranges, to make travel difficult. Of course, the Allegheny Plateau, covering eastern Ohio, has some rough hills and deep valleys, but beyond the Scioto River, the rest of the state is just gently rolling farmland. If you prefer water travel, Lake Erie and the Ohio River both provide excellent transportation routes. Every day, ships and barges make extensive use of these waterways, carrying raw materials to (and finished products from) Ohio's many factories. Because of these factories, Ohio ranks third in manufacturing jobs, trailing only California and Texas.

Between 1850 and 1950, Ohio's steel and machine-tool industries created good jobs that attracted immigrants from all over the world. Cleveland, for example, has had neighborhoods devoted to Germans, Irish, Poles, Italians, Czechs, Russians, Greeks, and also blacks who moved up from the South after the Civil War. However, as industry in Ohio grew unchecked, so did the presence of black smoke in the air and harmful chemicals in the water. Now that heavy industry in Ohio has declined, as it has elsewhere in the region, Ohioans must contend with the twin problems of pollution and unemployment.

One of the most unusual groups to have settled in Ohio are the Amish. A highly religious people, the Amish are known for their rejection of modern conveniences, such as cars and electricity, and for their excellent farming skills. Although many Amish live in Pennsylvania, the nation's largest Amish community is located in Holmes County near Millersburg.

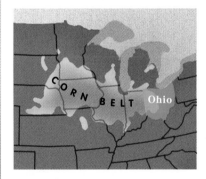

Ohio lies at the eastern end of the agricultural Corn Belt that stretches all the way west to Nebraska. Known to geographers as the Dissected Till Plains, this region was created thousands of years ago by glaciers that flattened the land and left behind fertile soil when they melted.

During the 1960s, the pollution became so bad in Lake Erie that it was declared "dead." Since then, environmental laws have stopped the dumping of untreated chemicals. As a result, fish have returned, and beaches have been reopened.

 Interstate Highways
⭐ State Capital
☐ Native American Reservations
National Forests
■ National Parks and Refuges
▲ Highest Point

0	miles	50
0	kilometers	80

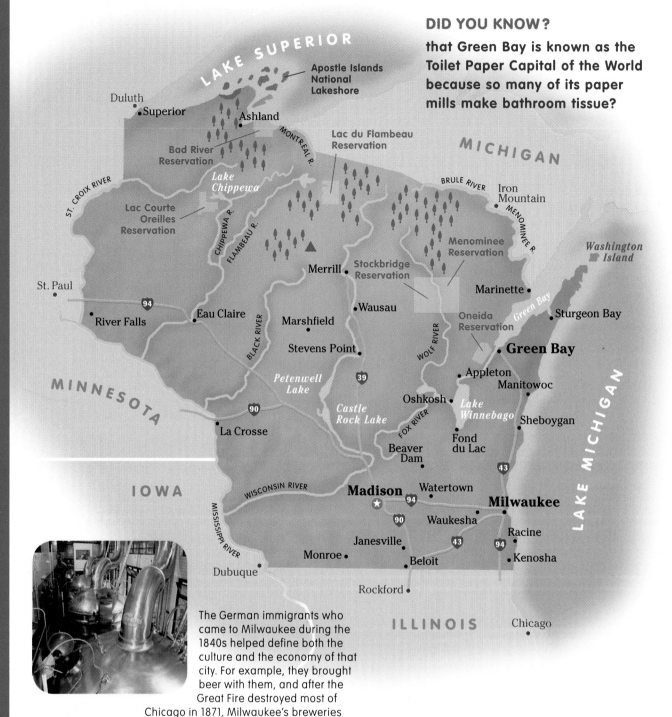

DID YOU KNOW?

that Green Bay is known as the Toilet Paper Capital of the World because so many of its paper mills make bathroom tissue?

LAKE SUPERIOR

Duluth
• Superior
Ashland •
Apostle Islands National Lakeshore

Bad River Reservation
MONTREAL R.

Lac du Flambeau Reservation

MICHIGAN

ST. CROIX RIVER

Lake Chippewa

BRULE RIVER
Iron Mountain

MENOMINEE R.

Lac Courte Oreilles Reservation

CHIPPEWA R.

FLAMBEAU R.

Menominee Reservation

Washington Island

St. Paul

Merrill •

Stockbridge Reservation

Marinette •

Green Bay

Sturgeon Bay

94

Eau Claire •
River Falls •

Marshfield •

Wausau •

Oneida Reservation

WOLF RIVER

Green Bay

MINNESOTA

BLACK RIVER

Stevens Point •

Appleton •

Manitowoc

39

Petenwell Lake

Oshkosh •

Lake Winnebago

Sheboygan

Castle Rock Lake

FOX RIVER

Fond du Lac •

90

La Crosse •

Beaver Dam •

43

LAKE MICHIGAN

IOWA

WISCONSIN RIVER

Madison ⭐

Watertown •

Milwaukee

MISSISSIPPI RIVER

94

90

Waukesha •

Racine •

Janesville •

43

94

Monroe •

Beloit •

Kenosha •

Dubuque

Rockford •

ILLINOIS

Chicago •

The German immigrants who came to Milwaukee during the 1840s helped define both the culture and the economy of that city. For example, they brought beer with them, and after the Great Fire destroyed most of Chicago in 1871, Milwaukee's breweries became the nation's most important.

◄———— **295 miles (475 km)** ————►

ABOUT WISCONSIN

NICKNAME: Badger State	**POPULATION:** 5,401,906 (18th)	**FLOWER:** Wood violet
CAPITAL: Madison	**AREA:** 65,499 sq. mi. (23rd)	**TREE:** Sugar maple
STATEHOOD: May 29, 1848 (30th)	(169,569 sq km)	**BIRD:** Robin
MOTTO: Forward.	**HIGHEST POINT:** 1,951 ft. (Timms Hill)	**FISH:** Muskellunge
	LOWEST POINT: 579 ft. (Lake Michigan)	

Wisconsin

WISCONSIN

1848

Wisconsin calls itself America's Dairyland with good reason: Its 1.3 million dairy cows are the most of any state. "Milking" this advantage, Wisconsin leads the nation in both butter and cheese making and places second (behind California) in overall milk production.

Most of Wisconsin's dairy farms are located in the southern two-thirds of the state. During the last Ice Age, glaciers flattened this area and enriched its soil. Curiously, though, the glaciers flowed around southwestern Wisconsin, creating a Driftless Area of steep valleys and narrow ridges that extends into Minnesota, Iowa, and Illinois. (Drift is glacial debris.) In the north, Wisconsin is mostly forested with second-growth trees that grew up naturally after older ones were cut down by settlers or harvested by paper companies.

Wisconsin's manufacturing industries and largest cities are concentrated in the southeast. The state's most successful paper mills, for example, are in the Fox and Wisconsin river valleys. Southeastern Wisconsin is also filled with many ethnic enclaves that reflect the state's history of heavy immigration from northern Europe. The Germans who arrived first were soon followed by Poles, Swedes, and Norwegians, among other groups. Today, Wisconsinites celebrate their cultural heritage with such annual events as the Wilhelm Tell Festival in New Glarus (Swiss), the Syttende Mai Festival in Stoughton (Norwegian), and the Fyr Bal Festival in Ephraim (Icelandic).

What the Kentucky Derby is to horse racing, the Oshkosh Fly-In is to aviation. Every summer, pilots from all over the world descend on Wittman Regional Airport in Oshkosh, flying more than ten thousand small aircraft. The occasion is the annual convention of the Experimental Aircraft Association.

Nearly 90 percent of the state's milk goes to cheese making, an industry promoted in Wisconsin by German, Swiss, and Norwegian immigrants more than a century ago.

The lakes and forests of Wisconsin's North Woods attract hunters and fishermen from all over the Midwest. Much of the land is protected by Wisconsin's environmental laws, among the most progressive in the nation.

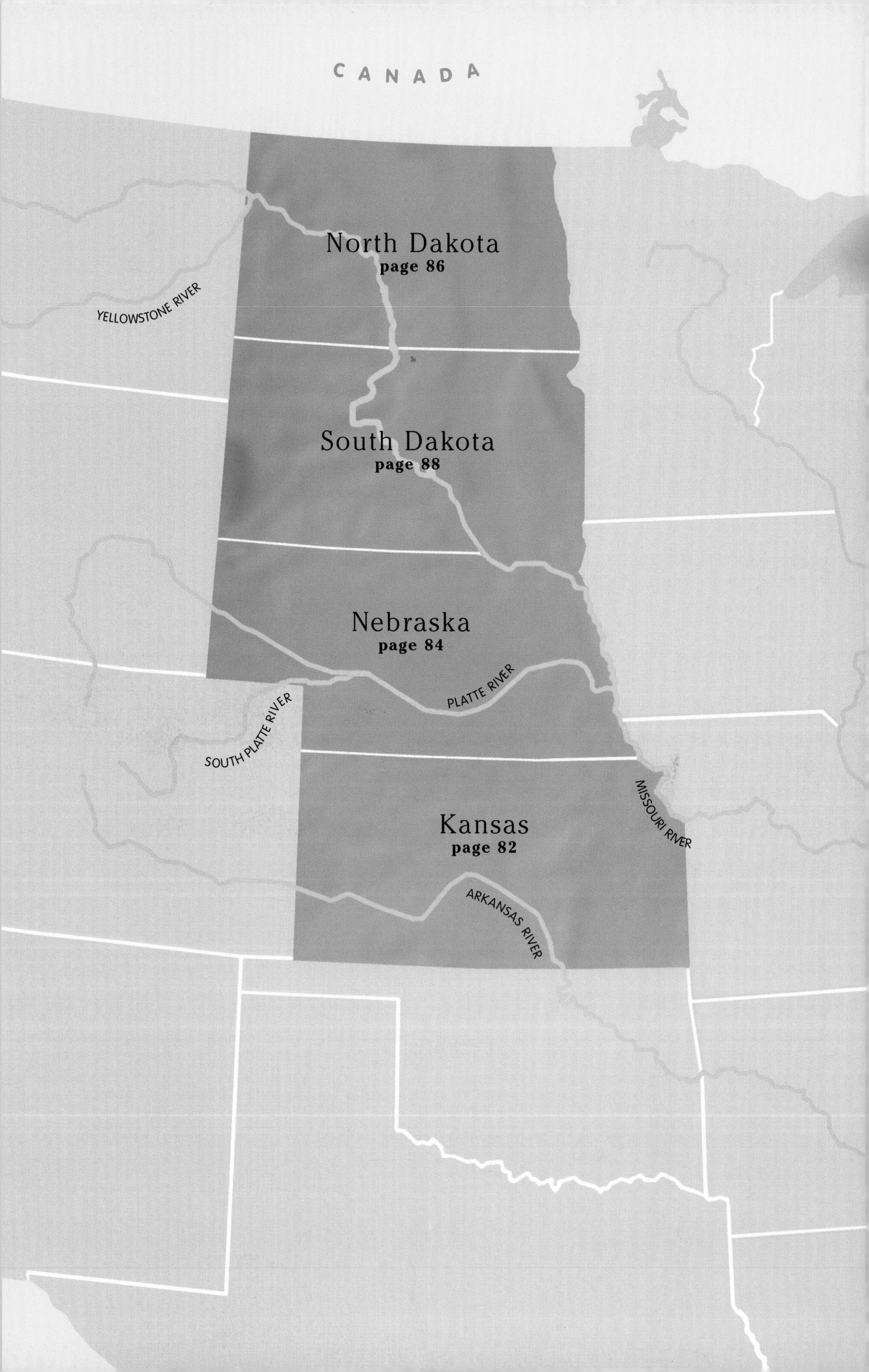

YELLOWSTONE RIVER

North Dakota
page 86

South Dakota
page 88

Nebraska
page 84

SOUTH PLATTE RIVER

PLATTE RIVER

MISSOURI RIVER

Kansas
page 82

ARKANSAS RIVER

CANADA

Great Plains

With no large body of water nearby to moderate the climate, the landlocked states of the Great Plains enjoy (or suffer from) some of the nation's most extreme weather. The summers are hot, the winters are cold and snowy, and the wind blows mightily year-round because there are few natural barriers (such as trees or hills) to block it. During spring and fall when air masses clash overhead, violent weather often results, and tornadoes are common.

LEGEND

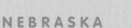

Interstate Highways	State Capital	Native American Reservations	National Parks and Refuges	Highest Point	0 / 0	miles / kilometers	100 / 161

DID YOU KNOW?

that the first newspaper in Kansas was published in the Shawnee language?

NEBRASKA

Lincoln

Kickapoo Reservation

Potowatomi Reservation

MISSOURI

MISSOURI R.

REPUBLICAN RIVER

Lebanon

Waconda Lake

SOLOMON RIVER

SMOKY HILLS

Tuttle Creek Lake

Atchison

Leavenworth

29

35

Goodland

SALINE RIVER

Milford Lake

Manhattan

KANSAS R.

Kansas City

70

Hays

Junction City

Topeka

Lawrence

70

Kansas City

SMOKY HILL RIVER

Salina

Abilene

Olathe

70

Cedar Bluff Reservoir

Cheyenne Bottoms

McPherson

335

Emporia

35

Great Bend

135

John Redmond Reservoir

COL.

Quivira National Wildlife Refuge

Newton

35

Fort Scott

Garden City

ARKANSAS RIVER

Dodge City

Hutchinson

Wichita

Cheney Reservoir

NEOSHOE RIVER

Ulysses

Pratt

FLINT HILLS

CIMARRON RIVER

RED HILLS

Wellington

Winfield

Liberal

Arkansas City

Coffeyville

35

OKLAHOMA

Tulsa

Wichita-area companies such as Raytheon and Learjet lead the world in the manufacture of light aircraft, making nearly two out of every three planes sold. Referring to his factory's midcountry location, aircraft executive Walter Beech once said, "No matter where you deliver an airplane from Wichita, you're already halfway there."

←————— 411 miles (661 km) —————→

ABOUT KANSAS

NICKNAME: Sunflower State

CAPITAL: Topeka

STATEHOOD: January 29, 1861 (34th)

MOTTO: To the stars through difficulties.

POPULATION: 2,694,641 (32nd)

AREA: 82,282 sq. mi. (15th) (213,018 sq km)

HIGHEST POINT: 4,039 ft. (Mount Sunflower)

LOWEST POINT: 679 ft. (Verdigris River)

FLOWER: Wild native sunflower

TREE: Cottonwood

BIRD: Western meadowlark

Kansas

Kansas seems to encourage misconceptions. For example, early pioneers believed that its dry, hard soil could never be farmed. Yet in 1874, a group of Russian Mennonite immigrants introduced a special strain of hardy winter wheat that required much less water than other wheats. This Turkey Red strain transformed Kansas into the nation's leading wheat producer.

Another misconception is that Kansas is primarily an agricultural state. That may once have been true, but modern methods of farming —especially the expensive new machinery that allows fewer and fewer people to farm more and more land—have undermined the state's small-town way of life. Looking elsewhere for work, many young families have left western and central Kansas for the industrialized eastern third of the state. This shift has left Kansas's small towns smaller and the average age of the people who live in them higher.

Some people even think that Kansas is flat! In fact, much of the state is covered with low hills. The Dissected Till Plains of northeastern Kansas and the Osage Plains in the extreme southeast are both areas of rolling hills and rich prairie soil. West of the Osage Plains are the Flint Hills, whose abundant bluestem grass provides some of the best grazing land in the country. Farther west are the gently rising Great Plains, which take up half of the state beginning near Tuttle Creek in the north and Hutchinson in the south.

During the early twentieth century, when William Allen White edited the *Emporia Gazette*, Kansas became internationally famous for its many excellent small-town newspapers. Even today, Kansas has more newspapers per capita than any other state.

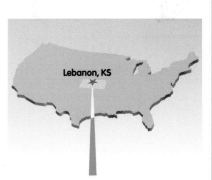

Truly Middle America
A limestone monument in a pasture just northeast of Lebanon marks the geographic center of the continental United States.

Although the wheat fields of central Kansas produce 15-20 percent of the annual U.S. harvest, farmers in the state make about twice as much money raising beef cattle in the Flint Hills and elsewhere.

LEGEND

🛡20 Interstate Highways	⭐ State Capital	Native American Reservations	🌲 National Forests	National Parks and Refuges	Grasslands	▲ Highest Point	0 ——— miles ——— 100		
							0 ——— kilometers ——— 161		

DID YOU KNOW?

that Interstate 80, which follows the same route taken by the Oregon Trail and the first transcontinental railroad, remains the nation's busiest east-west highway?

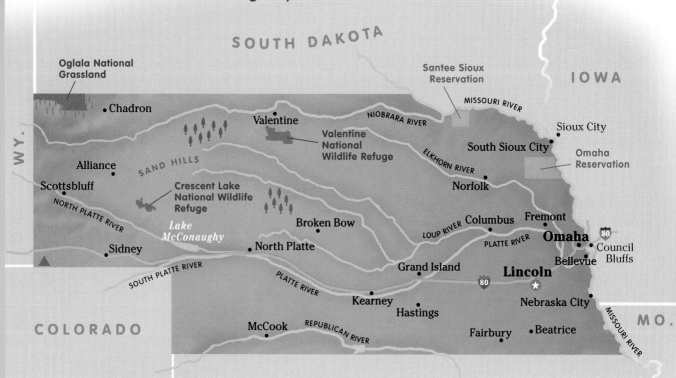

SOUTH DAKOTA

IOWA

- Oglala National Grassland
- Chadron
- Valentine
- Santee Sioux Reservation
- MISSOURI RIVER
- NIOBRARA RIVER
- Sioux City
- Valentine National Wildlife Refuge
- South Sioux City
- Omaha Reservation
- ELKHORN RIVER
- Alliance
- SAND HILLS
- Norfolk
- Scottsbluff
- NORTH PLATTE RIVER
- Crescent Lake National Wildlife Refuge
- Lake McConaughy
- Broken Bow
- Columbus
- Fremont
- LOUP RIVER
- Omaha
- PLATTE RIVER
- Council Bluffs
- Sidney
- North Platte
- Bellevue
- Grand Island
- Lincoln ⭐
- SOUTH PLATTE RIVER
- PLATTE RIVER
- Kearney
- Nebraska City
- Hastings
- McCook
- REPUBLICAN RIVER
- Fairbury
- Beatrice
- MISSOURI RIVER

WY.

COLORADO

KANSAS

MO.

Although agriculture remains important to Nebraskans, the state economy has diversified in recent years. For example, Omaha was once a national center for meatpacking. Now the most prosperous companies in town are insurance companies and telemarketers.

◄——————— 415 miles (668 km) ———————►

ABOUT NEBRASKA

NICKNAME: Cornhusker State

CAPITAL: Lincoln

STATEHOOD: March 1, 1867 (37th)

MOTTO: Equality before the law.

POPULATION: 1,713,235 (38th)

AREA: 77,358 sq. mi. (16th)
(200,271 sq km)

HIGHEST POINT: 5,424 ft. (Johnson Township)

LOWEST POINT: 840 ft. (Missouri River)

FLOWER: Goldenrod

TREE: Cottonwood

BIRD: Western meadowlark

Nebraska

The nineteenth-century homesteaders who settled Nebraska came out west to farm. At first, they concentrated themselves in the Platte River Valley, along the route of the Oregon Trail, where water was readily available. Then, as the use of irrigation expanded, they settled other parts of the state, once considered a Great American Desert by early explorers.

Today, agriculture has become such a universal way of life in Nebraska that farms and ranches occupy 94 percent of the land, the highest percentage of any state. In western Nebraska, wheat fields flow uninterrupted to the horizon, while farmers in the east grow corn, the state's best-known and most important crop. Ranching is also profitable in Nebraska, which ranks third behind Texas and Kansas in beef cattle production.

Nearly all Nebraska lies on the Great Plains, which begin near the junction of the Loup and Platte rivers. (The eastern edge of the state belongs to the Dissected Till Plains.) The terrain, mostly featureless, rises from east to west, but so gradually that it seems flat. Only near the Colorado border does the land give way to the buttes and valleys characteristic of the High Plains. One notable exception are the Sand Hills of north-central Nebraska, the largest sand dune area in North America. The soil there is held in place by grasses that also provide excellent forage for cattle.

They call it Huskermania. The University of Nebraska football team, nicknamed the Cornhuskers, has sold out every one of its home games since November 3, 1962. During those games, Memorial Stadium in Lincoln, seating 72,700 people, becomes—all by itself—the third largest city in the state.

Nebraska's Ogallala Aquifer sits at the northern end of the High Plains Aquifer, the nation's largest underground reservoir. Water pumped from the Ogallala Aquifer allows Nebraska farmers to irrigate more than seven million acres (about 3 million ha), the most irrigated land in any state after California and Texas.

The surveyors who laid out Nebraska (and most of the Great Plains) used a strict rectangular grid system. Townships were built up from square 640-acre (259-hectare) "sections," with the basic unit of settlement being the quarter-section farm.

Interstate Highways State Capital Native American Reservations National Parks and Refuges Grasslands Highest Point

| 0 | miles | 100 |
| 0 | kilometers | 161 |

North Dakota typically ranks second behind Kansas in wheat production, yet every few years a particularly good harvest can nudge the state into first place. The two principal varieties grown in North Dakota are hard red spring wheat, used for making bread dough, and durum, from which spaghetti is made.

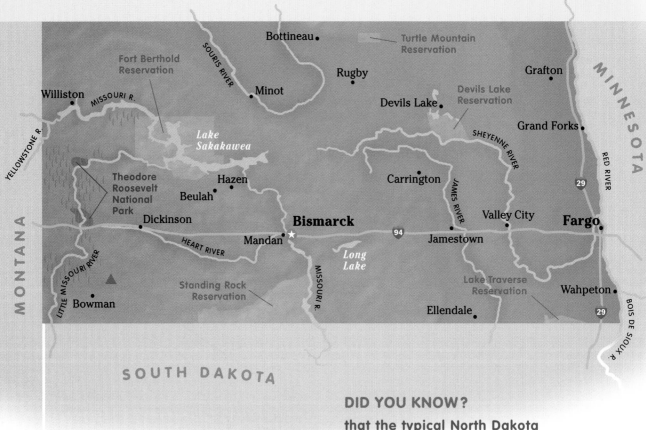

CANADA

Bottineau

Turtle Mountain Reservation

Fort Berthold Reservation

SOURIS RIVER

Rugby

Grafton

MINNESOTA

Williston

MISSOURI R.

Minot

Devils Lake

Devils Lake Reservation

Grand Forks

SHEYENNE RIVER

RED RIVER

YELLOWSTONE R.

Lake Sakakawea

Theodore Roosevelt National Park

Hazen

Beulah

Carrington

JAMES RIVER

Valley City

29

Dickinson

Bismarck

94

Jamestown

Fargo

MONTANA

Mandan

HEART RIVER

MISSOURI R.

Long Lake

LITTLE MISSOURI RIVER

Standing Rock Reservation

Lake Traverse Reservation

Wahpeton

BOIS DE SIOUX R.

Bowman

Ellendale

29

SOUTH DAKOTA

DID YOU KNOW?

that the typical North Dakota farmer grows enough food each year to feed 129 people for a year (up from 26 people in 1960)?

◄---------------- 360 miles (579 km) ----------------►

ABOUT NORTH DAKOTA

NICKNAME: Peace Garden State

CAPITAL: Bismarck

STATEHOOD: November 2, 1889 (39th)

MOTTO: Liberty and union, now and forever, one and inseparable.

POPULATION: 634,448 (48th)

AREA: 70,704 sq. mi. (19th) (183,044 sq km)

HIGHEST POINT: 3,506 ft. (White Butte)

LOWEST POINT: 750 ft. (Red River)

FLOWER: Wild prairie rose

TREE: American elm

BIRD: Western meadowlark

FISH: Northern pike

North Dakota

Many North Dakotans have a lively sense of humor about their state. They tell jokes like "You know you're a North Dakotan if you define *summer* as three months of bad sledding." The climate there can indeed be challenging: Far from the moderating influence of an ocean and without trees or hills for windbreaks, North Dakota experiences some of the continent's hottest and coldest temperatures, not to mention frequent dust storms and blizzards. The weather, combined with the state's small population and apparently endless prairie landscape, might make a less hardy people lonely. Yet North Dakotans pride themselves on their positive outlook and spirit of cooperation.

Most of the businesses in the state depend on agriculture. The rich soil supports an abundance of wheat as well as the largest barley, flax, pinto bean, and sunflower crops in the country. Farms tend to be large, nearly three times the national average, which is why North Dakotans live so far apart. The state's tiny manufacturing sector is generally confined to the larger cities, where most of the factories process food—the pasta-making plant in Fargo, for instance, and the sugar beet refineries in Grand Forks.

Fargo and Grand Forks are located in the extremely fertile Red River Valley on the eastern edge of the state. The next regions over are the Drift Prairie and then the Missouri Plateau, a hilly and stony part of the Great Plains that covers the entire western half of North Dakota.

Because so many North Dakotans live in isolated areas, less than half the population has access to a library. To meet this need, most county libraries have established bookmobile programs to service rural areas.

Ice Age glaciers carved North Dakota into a series of stepped plateaus. From the Red River Valley, once the bottom of a huge glacial lake, the land rises sharply to the Drift Prairie (which takes its name from the glacial debris called drift). A similar step separates the Drift Prairie from the Missouri Plateau.

North Dakota has plenty of prairie grass but not much shade. Of the fifty states, it has the lowest percentage of forested land, only about 1 percent. The few trees that do grow there are mostly found in the Turtle Mountains.

LEGEND

20	★					▲	0	miles	100
Interstate Highways	State Capital	Native American Reservations	National Forests	National Parks and Refuges	Grasslands	Highest Point	0	kilometers	161

During the early 1980s, Citibank became the single largest employer in Sioux Falls when it moved its credit-card operations there. Since then, other financial services companies have followed, bringing more jobs and transforming Sioux Falls into an important center for credit-card processing.

NORTH DAKOTA

MONTANA

Standing Rock Reservation

Lake Traverse Reservation

Wahpeton

BOIS DE SIOUX R.

Lake Traverse

Buffalo

GRAND RIVER

Mobridge

Aberdeen

Waubay Lake

Big Stone Lake

MOREAU RIVER

Cheyenne River Reservation

Redfield

Watertown

BELLE FOURCHE RIVER

CHEYENNE RIVER

Lake Oahe

Crow Creek Reservation

JAMES RIVER

Lake Poinsett

29

MINNESOTA

Sturgis

BLACK HILLS

Pierre ★

Huron

Brookings

Badlands National Park

Rapid City

BAD RIVER

Mount Rushmore National Memorial

90

WHITE RIVER

Mitchell

Sioux Falls •

Hot Springs

Pine Ridge Reservation

Rosebud Reservation

Winner

Lake Francis Case

MISSOURI RIVER

BIG SIOUX R.

29

IOWA

Pine Ridge

Wind Cave National Park

WYOMING

NEBRASKA

Yankton Reservation

Yankton

•Vermillion

• Sioux City

MISSOURI RIVER

DID YOU KNOW?

that South Dakota has more free-roaming buffalo, approximately thirty thousand head, than any other state?

◄———— 380 miles (611 km) ————►

ABOUT SOUTH DAKOTA

NICKNAME: Mount Rushmore State

CAPITAL: Pierre

STATEHOOD: November 2, 1889 (40th)

MOTTO: Under God the people rule.

POPULATION: 756,600 (46th)

AREA: 77,121 sq. mi. (17th) (199,659 sq km)

HIGHEST POINT: 7,242 ft. (Harney Peak)

LOWEST POINT: 966 ft. (Big Stone Lake)

FLOWER: Pasqueflower

TREE: Black Hills spruce

BIRD: Ring-necked pheasant

FISH: Walleye

South Dakota

South Dakotans seem to live by two simple rules: Where the soil is fertile, you plant crops. Where the grass grows high, you raise livestock. In all, 91 percent of the land in the state is devoted to agriculture. In the fields of the east, farmers grow corn, wheat, hay, and other crops; in the grazing lands of the west, ranchers raise cattle, hogs, and sheep.

However, the Native Americans who live on South Dakota's many reservations are often unable to share in this agricultural prosperity. The reasons are mostly historical. For instance, the reservations onto which their ancestors were confined during the 1870s included some of the least arable land in the state. Nevertheless, many Sioux and Cheyenne leaders, while working hard to preserve ancient traditions, have helped their people find suitable modern lifestyles.

Winding among these reservations, the Missouri River is South Dakota's major geographical landmark. East of the river lies the Drift Prairie, where ancient glaciers left behind excellent farmland. Most South Dakotans live on this side of the river, on farms and in small towns. West of the Missouri, untouched by the glaciers that smoothed the eastern bank, are the dry, treeless grasslands of the Great Plains. Except for the area around the Black Hills, there are so few people in western South Dakota (an average of only three per square mile) that the land seems nearly deserted.

Native Americans, most of them Sioux, make up 8.3 percent of the South Dakota population. (Only Alaska and New Mexico have higher percentages.) Like many other nations, the Oglala Sioux, who live on the Pine Ridge Reservation, hold an annual powwow to celebrate their cultural heritage with craft displays and dancing competitions.

South Dakota has been so successful at promoting itself that tourism now ranks just behind agriculture in the state economy. One of the most popular sights is the quartet of presidential busts carved into the Black Hills at Mount Rushmore. Each head stands as tall as a six-story building.

Rising above southwestern South Dakota is a range of granite cliffs. The Sioux call this land Paha Sapa. Others call it the Black Hills because thick pine forests make the region look much darker than the surrounding plain.

CANADA

MISSOURI RIVER

Montana
page 96

YELLOWSTONE RIVER

Idaho
page 94

SNAKE RIVER

Wyoming
page 100

NORTH PLATTE RIVER

Utah
page 98

Colorado
page 92

SOUTH PLATTE RIVER

COLORADO RIVER

RIO GRANDE

ARKANSAS RIVER

CANADA

MEXICO

Mountain

90

L ike the Appalachians, the Rocky Mountains that tower over this region are, in fact, a series of distinct ranges, such as the Wasatch Range in Utah and the Bitterroots in Montana. These ranges are separated from one another by river valleys. Nearly all of the West's great rivers begin in the Rockies. The Arkansas, Colorado, Missouri, Platte, and Rio Grande all have sources at or near the Continental Divide, the ridgeline that separates the drainage basins of the Pacific and Atlantic oceans.

Mountain

Interstate Highways

 State Capital

Native American Reservations

National Forests

National Parks and Refuges

Grasslands

▲ Highest Point

0	miles	100
0	kilometers	161

Colorado Springs, the home of the Air Force Academy, is the center of the state's robust defense and aerospace industries. Just south of town, for example, inside hollowed-out Cheyenne Mountain, the North American Aerospace Defense Command (NORAD) monitors U.S. and Canadian airspace for incoming aircraft and missiles.

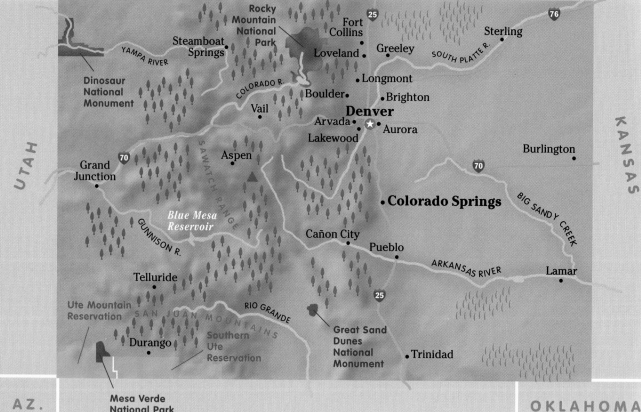

WYOMING

NEBRASKA

Cheyenne

Rocky Mountain National Park

Fort Collins

25

Sterling

76

Steamboat Springs

YAMPA RIVER

Loveland

Greeley

SOUTH PLATTE R.

Dinosaur National Monument

COLORADO R.

Longmont

Boulder

Brighton

Vail

Denver ★

UTAH

Arvada

Aurora

Lakewood

Burlington

Grand Junction

70

Aspen

SAWATCH RANGE

70

KANSAS

Colorado Springs

Blue Mesa Reservoir

GUNNISON R.

Cañon City

BIG SANDY CREEK

Pueblo

Telluride

SAN JUAN MOUNTAINS

RIO GRANDE

ARKANSAS RIVER

Lamar

Ute Mountain Reservation

Durango

Southern Ute Reservation

25

Great Sand Dunes National Monument

Trinidad

AZ.

Mesa Verde National Park

OKLAHOMA

Taos

DID YOU KNOW?

that the lowest point in Colorado is higher than the highest point in eighteen states?

NEW MEXICO

TEXAS

◄———— 387 miles (623 km) ————►

ABOUT COLORADO

NICKNAME: Centennial State

CAPITAL: Denver

STATEHOOD: August 1, 1876 (38th)

MOTTO: Nothing without providence.

POPULATION: 4,417,714 (24th)

AREA: 104,100 sq. mi. (8th)
(269,503 sq km)

HIGHEST POINT: 14,433 ft. (Mount Elbert)

LOWEST POINT: 3,350 ft. (Arkansas River)

FLOWER: Rocky Mountain columbine

TREE: Blue spruce

BIRD: Lark bunting

Colorado

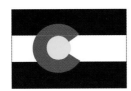

More than in other states, the culture wars of the early twenty-first century are being fought in Colorado. On one side are the old-time, highly conservative, business-oriented Coloradans. On the other are environmentally conscious liberals, many of whom emigrated from California during the 1970s and 1980s. Lately, however, an influx of well-paid high-tech workers has shifted the political balance again, this time to the more conservative side, especially on such hot topics as the Rocky Mountains and whether they should be mined or protected.

The Rockies still support a profitable mining industry, and cattle ranches still cover the High Plains, yet the state's economy no longer depends so heavily on natural resources. Instead, as Colorado has become more multicultural, its economy has diversified as well, and light manufacturing—of scientific instruments, for example—has flourished. Colorado's recent economic boom has focused on the string of cities, from Pueblo north to Fort Collins, that line the eastern foothills of the Rockies. Most of the new money has concentrated here, as well as three quarters of the population.

Although Colorado is closely identified with the southern Rockies, much of the state happens to be flat. The eastern two-fifths belongs to the Great Plains, which rise gently from the Kansas border. The Rockies take up the central two-fifths, while the western fringe sits atop the Colorado Plateau. Wind and water have eroded this upland into a scenic maze of canyons and flat-topped hills called mesas.

Each winter, twelve million people visit Colorado's world-famous ski resorts. Among the most glamorous of these are Aspen and Vail. (Vail also happens to be the largest ski resort in North America.) Thanks to state-of-the-art snowmaking machines, the ski season begins as early as October and continues for eight months.

COLORADO IN CROSS SECTION

14,000 ft. / 4,267 m

12,000 ft. / 3,658 m

10,000 ft. / 3,048 m

8,000 ft. / 2,438 m

Mean Altitude: 6,800 ft. / 2,073 m

6,000 ft. / 1,829 m

4,000 ft. / 1,219 m

2,000 ft. / 610 m

Rocky Mountain High
Colorado's mean altitude of sixty-eight hundred feet is the highest of any state. Nationwide, there are ninety-one peaks above fourteen thousand feet. Of these ninety-one "fourteeners," fifty-six are in Colorado.

With Colorado's growth, Denver has become the transportation and financial center of the Mountain West. It's called the Mile High City because it sits at an average elevation of 5,280 feet (1,609 m).

Interstate Highways | State Capital | Native American Reservations | National Forests | National Parks and Refuges | Highest Point

0 miles 100
0 kilometers 161

CANADA

Priest Lake

Sandpoint

WASH.

Lake Pend Oreille

Spokane

Coeur d'Alene

Kellog — 90

Coeur d'Alene Reservation

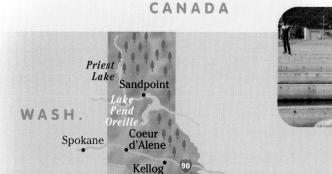

Clear Springs Foods, headquartered near Twin Falls, is the world's leading producer of aqua-cultured rainbow trout. Altogether, companies in south-central Idaho produce about 75 percent of the food-size trout sold in the United States. The fish are raised in ponds cooled by underground springs.

Moscow

CLEARWATER RIVER

Missoula

Nez Perce Reservation

Lewiston

S. FORK CLEARWATER R.

SELWAY RIVER

Butte

DID YOU KNOW?

that the wiggle in Idaho's otherwise straight western border is Hells Canyon, the continent's deepest river-carved gorge?

Grangeville

CLEARWATER MTS.

SALMON RIVER

MONTANA

Salmon

SNAKE RIVER

SALMON RIVER MTS.

SAWTOOTH MTS.

Yellowstone National Park

Craters of the Moon National Monument

Rexburg

15

Sun Valley

Caldwell

★ **Boise**

Ketchum

Nampa

Hailey

Idaho Falls

WYO.

Mountain Home

SNAKE RIVER PLAIN

Grays Lake

84

American Falls Reservoir

Fort Hall Reservation

Pocatello

OREGON

Duck Valley Reservation

86

Twin Falls

Burley

15

Bear Lake

84

Preston

NEVADA

UTAH

Logan

◄— 305 miles (491 km) —►

ABOUT IDAHO

NICKNAME: Gem State
CAPITAL: Boise
STATEHOOD: July 3, 1890 (43rd)
MOTTO: Let it be perpetual.

POPULATION: 1,321,006 (39th)
AREA: 83,574 sq. mi. (14th)
(216,363 sq km)
HIGHEST POINT: 12,662 ft. (Borah Peak)
LOWEST POINT: 710 ft. (Snake River)

FLOWER: Syringa
TREE: Western white pine
BIRD: Mountain bluebird
FISH: Cutthroat trout

Idaho

The Idaho Potato Commission spends bushels and bushels of money each year to make certain that the words *Idaho* and *potato* remain closely linked in the American mind. In return, the Idaho potato industry generates $2.5 billion a year, or 15 percent of the state's gross product, which is no small potatoes.

Yet to dismiss Idaho as a single giant potato farm would be wrong. For one thing, the many potato farms there are crowded into just one small section of the state, the Snake River Plain, which is Idaho's only level ground. Elsewhere, the state is a wilderness of forests and mountains, including some of the country's most rugged and least accessible land. Residents of the Idaho Panhandle, in particular, tend to be independent and self-reliant, because they have no other choice.

Although Idaho, like most mountain states, has some mineral and timber resources, environmentally conscious residents are much more interested in developing the state's wilderness tourism industry. For example, thanks to federal protection, the Salmon and Clearwater rivers have both become meccas for white-water rafters.

Except for isolated timber and mining settlements, most towns in Idaho follow the course of the Snake River, and most people live on the Snake River Plain atop the Columbia Plateau. Aside from a lip of the Great Basin jutting into the state from Utah, the rest of Idaho—specifically, the northern two-thirds—belongs to the Rocky Mountains.

At the World Center for Birds of Prey in Boise, the Peregrine Fund houses over two hundred endangered hunting birds, including California condors, harpy eagles, and Aplomado falcons. An international leader in endangered species research, the center breeds these birds in captivity, then releases their young into the wild.

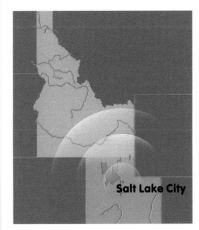

Salt Lake City

After Utah, Idaho has the highest concentration of Mormons, or members of the Church of Jesus Christ of Latter-day Saints. State-wide, Mormons make up about 27 percent of the population. However, near the Utah border in Idaho's desert southeast, many towns are as much as 90 percent Mormon.

Idaho boasts eighteen million acres (about 7 million ha) of wilderness, the most of any state after Alaska. In fact, some parts of the mountainous, heavily forested Panhandle have remained essentially unchanged since Lewis and Clark explored them in 1805.

🛣 20 Interstate Highways

⭐ State Capital

🟩 Native American Reservations

🌲 National Forests

🟫 National Parks and Refuges

🔺 Highest Point

| 0 | miles | 100 |
| 0 | kilometers | 161 |

Nearly all the manufacturing in Montana makes use of the state's natural resources. For example, lumber and wood products such as pencils and telephone poles account for about one third of the state's total output. The rest are mostly oil, coal, metal, and food products.

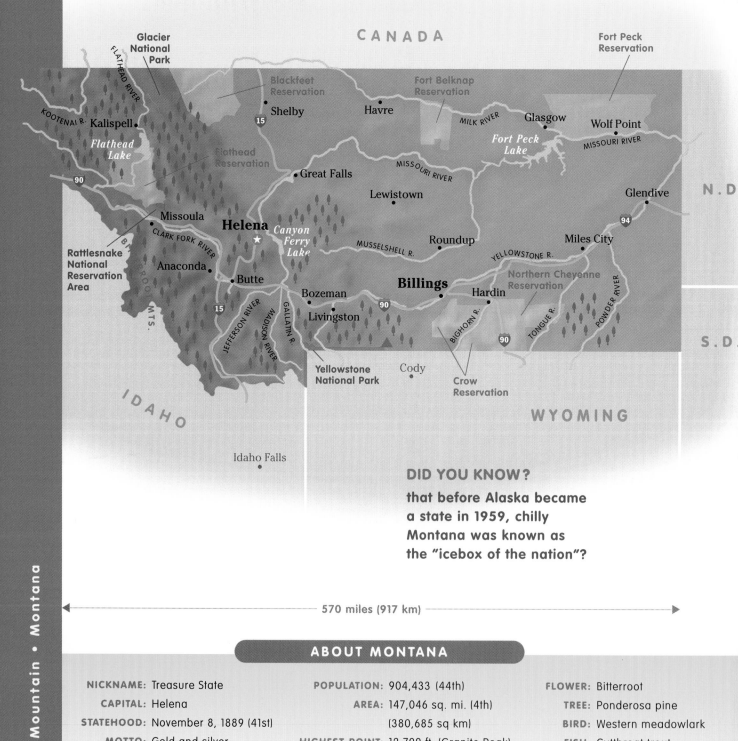

CANADA

Glacier National Park

FLATHEAD RIVER

KOOTENAI R. Kalispell

Flathead Lake

Flathead Reservation

Blackfeet Reservation

Shelby

Havre

Fort Belknap Reservation

MILK RIVER

Glasgow

Fort Peck Lake

Fort Peck Reservation

Wolf Point

MISSOURI RIVER

90

Missoula

Great Falls

MISSOURI RIVER

Lewistown

Glendive

N. D

Helena

CLARK FORK RIVER

Canyon Ferry Lake

94

Rattlesnake National Reservation Area

Anaconda

Butte

MUSSELSHELL R.

Roundup

Miles City

Northern Cheyenne Reservation

YELLOWSTONE R.

BITTERROOT MTS.

15

JEFFERSON RIVER

MADISON RIVER

GALLATIN R.

Bozeman

Livingston

90

Billings

Hardin

BIGHORN R.

TONGUE R.

POWDER RIVER

S. D.

90

Yellowstone National Park

Cody

Crow Reservation

IDAHO

WYOMING

Idaho Falls

DID YOU KNOW?

that before Alaska became a state in 1959, chilly Montana was known as the "icebox of the nation"?

◄———————— 570 miles (917 km) ————————►

ABOUT MONTANA

NICKNAME: Treasure State

CAPITAL: Helena

STATEHOOD: November 8, 1889 (41st)

MOTTO: Gold and silver.

POPULATION: 904,433 (44th)

AREA: 147,046 sq. mi. (4th)
(380,685 sq km)

HIGHEST POINT: 12,799 ft. (Granite Peak)

LOWEST POINT: 1,800 ft. (Kootenai River)

FLOWER: Bitterroot

TREE: Ponderosa pine

BIRD: Western meadowlark

FISH: Cutthroat trout

Montana

There are so few Montanans that parts of the state, the fourth largest, seem uninhabited. Attracted by this solitude, more and more celebrities have been buying ranches there to get away from it all. Meanwhile, the people who live there don't seem to take much notice. They're mostly cattle ranchers and wheat farmers, though a good number work for mining companies. The state's gold, silver, and copper supplies have largely run out, but oil, coal, and natural gas have taken their place.

As oil drilling and coal mining have expanded, they've become more controversial, especially among Montana's Native Americans. (The largest group after whites, they make up 6 percent of the state's population.) Most Native Americans living on Montana reservations urgently need the jobs and income mining would provide. However, many reservation leaders worry that exploiting these resources might permanently damage the environment.

Montana is called Big Sky Country because in the eastern two-thirds of the state, where the land is flat and open, it's easy to see a lot of sky. Buttes and small mountain ranges occasionally interrupt this treeless Great Plains grassland, but they seem insignificant compared with the Rocky Mountains of western Montana, along whose backbone runs the Continental Divide. In general, rain that falls on the western side of this divide runs into the Pacific Ocean, while rain that falls on its eastern side drains into the Atlantic.

Life in Montana is strongly oriented toward the outdoors. One reason is that the hunting and fishing there are exceptional: The Yellowstone River, for example, offers some of the best fly-fishing in the world.

Chinook Winds

Chinooks are unusually warm, dry winds that blow down from the Rockies every so often during winter. They can raise the air temperature 40°F (22°C) in less than an hour and melt enough snow so that cattle can graze— at least until the next snowfall.

Western Montana includes some of the most difficult and out-of-the-way territory in the country. There are mountains in Glacier National Park so steep and remote that no one has ever climbed them.

LEGEND

Interstate Highways
State Capital
Native American Reservations
National Forests
National Parks and Refuges
Highest Point

| 0 | miles | 100 |
| 0 | kilometers | 161 |

IDAHO

Bear Lake

BEAR R.

84
15

Logan

Brigham City

WYOMING

Ogden

Great Salt Lake

GREAT SALT LAKE DESERT

BONNEVILLE SALT FLATS

84
80

Salt Lake City ★

UINTA MOUNTAINS

80

Tooele •

• Sandy

• Orem

Dinosaur National Monument

Goshute Reservation

• Provo

Utah Lake

Uintah and Ouray Reservation

COLORADO

SEVIER DESERT

15

NEVADA

Delta •

SEVIER RIVER

Price •

WASATCH RANGE

GREEN RIVER

Ely •

Grand Junction

Richfield •

70

Moab •

Arches National Park

SAN RAFAEL DESERT

Canyonlands National Park

COLORADO RIVER

15

Cedar City •

Bryce Canyon National Park

Blanding •

Zion National Park

St. George •

SAN JUAN RIVER

MONUMENT VALLEY

Navajo Reservation

Lake Powell

N.M.

The federal government does a lot of its rocket shopping in Utah. The most important of its contractors there is Thiokol Propulsion, the world's largest producer of rocket engines. Thiokol makes reusable engines for the space shuttle as well as the motors used to launch Trident II and Minuteman nuclear missiles.

DID YOU KNOW?

that the Mormon church originally wanted to call the state Deseret, a name from the Book of Mormon that means "land of honeybees"?

ARIZONA

← 275 miles (442 km) →

ABOUT UTAH

NICKNAME: Beehive State
CAPITAL: Salt Lake City
STATEHOOD: January 4, 1896 (45th)
MOTTO: Industry.

POPULATION: 2,269,789 (34th)
AREA: 84,904 sq. mi. (13th)
(219,806 sq km)
HIGHEST POINT: 13,528 ft. (Kings Peak)
LOWEST POINT: 2,000 ft. (Beaverdam Wash)

FLOWER: Sego lily
TREE: Blue spruce
BIRD: California seagull
FISH: Bonneville cutthroat trout

Utah

The U.S. Constitution demands a separation between church and state. Yet it's difficult to imagine Utah without the Mormon church, also known as the Church of Jesus Christ of Latter-day Saints. A group of Mormons led by Brigham Young settled Utah in 1847, and Mormons still make up 70 percent of the population. Although the Mormon church no longer governs the state, it continues to play an important role in Utah's social life and institutions. For example, the Mormon preference for large families has kept the Utah birthrate well above the national average.

The Mormons were allowed to claim Utah, the nation's second driest state (after Nevada), largely because no other settlers wanted it. Most of the land, though geologically spectacular, cannot be farmed. What little arable land there is sits in a narrow band at the foot of the Wasatch Mountains, where streams fed by snowmelt carry water and mineral sediments down from the Rockies. As a result, about 80 percent of the population lives along the Wasatch Front between Provo and Ogden.

In the Rockies, the biggest business is mining, primarily gold, silver, and lead. To the south and east, the mountains flatten out into the Colorado Plateau, which covers slightly more than half the state. In this scenic region, featuring Zion and Bryce Canyon national parks, tourism is the most important industry. The western third of Utah belongs to the Great Basin and contains the Sevier and Great Salt Lake deserts as well as some of the flattest land on the continent.

Among Christians, Mormons are remarkable for having many beliefs uniquely their own, including their emphasis on business. To finance extensive missionary activities, the Mormon church runs many for-profit companies, including a department-store chain, an insurance company, and a "citrus ranch" in Florida.

The Great Salt Lake is all that's left of a huge freshwater lake that once covered western Utah. This ancient body of water, Lake Bonneville, was about the size that Lake Michigan is today. However, when the surrounding land rose, Lake Bonneville dried up, leaving the Great Salt Lake behind.

Southern Utah boasts some of the most spectacular rock formations on the North American continent. The buttes of Monument Valley may look familiar because they've appeared in many classic Hollywood westerns.

LEGEND

⟨20⟩ Interstate Highways	✪ State Capital	▢ Native American Reservations	🌲 National Forests	▦ National Parks and Refuges	🌾 Grasslands	▲ Highest Point	0 — miles — 100		
							0 — kilometers — 161		

Oil is the most valuable mineral in Wyoming, which produces about ninety million barrels of crude each year. This amount ranks the state fourth nationally behind Texas, Louisiana, and California. Many economists believe that Wyoming's future will depend increasingly on mining—particularly its reserves of oil, coal, and natural gas.

MONTANA

Yellowstone National Park

Yellowstone R.

Powell

Cody

Yellowstone Lake

Grand Teton National Park

Jackson

SNAKE RIVER

IDAHO

Wind River Reservation

WIND RIVER

Worland

Thermopolis

BIGHORN RIVER

BIG HORN MOUNTAINS

Sheridan

Buffalo

POWDER RIVER

Gillette

BELLE FOURCHE RIVER

Newcastle

SOUTH DAKOTA

WIND RIVER RANGE

Riverton

Lander

SWEETWATER RIVER

GREEN RIVER

Kemmerer

Green River

Rock Springs

Evanston

Flaming Gorge Reservoir

GREAT DIVIDE BASIN

Pathfinder Reservoir

Rawlins

NORTH PLATTE RIVER

Casper

Douglas

Seminoe Reservoir

MEDICINE BOW MOUNTAINS

MEDICINE BOW R.

LARAMIE R.

Torrington

Wheatland

NEBRASKA

Laramie

Cheyenne

⟨80⟩

⟨25⟩

UTAH

COLORADO

Denver

DID YOU KNOW?

that the 308-foot (94-meter) Lower Falls of the Yellowstone River is twice the height of Niagara Falls?

◄----------- 365 miles (587 km) -----------►

ABOUT WYOMING

NICKNAME: Equality State
CAPITAL: Cheyenne
STATEHOOD: July 10, 1890 (44th)
MOTTO: Equal rights.

POPULATION: 494,423 (50th)
AREA: 97,818 sq. mi. (10th)
(253,239 sq km)
HIGHEST POINT: 13,804 ft. (Gannett Peak)
LOWEST POINT: 3,099 ft. (Belle Fourche River)

FLOWER: Indian paintbrush
TREE: Plains cottonwood
BIRD: Meadowlark
FISH: Cutthroat trout

Wyoming

Famous for its scenic beauty, Wyoming attracts nearly five million tourists a year. Many come to visit Yellowstone and Grand Teton national parks, yet few stay. The population of Wyoming, despite its large size, is the lowest of any state in the Union, perhaps because life on its dry plains and in its rugged mountains can be so difficult.

Most of the people who live in Wyoming are the descendants of the whites, Mexicans, and Native Americans who originally settled the land. The state's many ranches and rodeos give the impression that Wyoming is the last refuge of the American cowboy. In fact, many Wyoming ranchers have to hire cowboys from Mexico, Chile, and Peru to do this hard, lonesome work.

Ranching and other farming activities generate $900 million a year for Wyoming, yet agriculture ranks a distant third in the state economy. Mining is far and away Wyoming's biggest business, at $4.7 billion per year (with tourism second). In addition to its plentiful oil, Wyoming has huge coal reserves, the nation's largest, enough to last more than three hundred years.

Only the eastern fringe of Wyoming lies on the Great Plains. The rest of the state, which straddles the Continental Divide, belongs to the Rocky Mountains. Separating Wyoming's many ranges are the dry flat-lands of the Intermontane Basin. Much of Wyoming's mineral wealth rests beneath these high, cold plateaus, whose short-grass prairies provide excellent grazing for the state's largest cattle ranches.

Cheyenne began hosting its annual Frontier Days celebration in 1897. The rodeo was the brainchild of a Union Pacific railroad agent who wanted to promote his trains but needed a destination. Today, more than twelve hundred cowboys and cowgirls take part in the roping, riding, and steer-wrestling competitions.

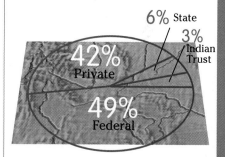

The federal government still owns a great deal of land in the West. For example, it owns 49 percent of Wyoming and more than half of western Montana.

Compared to the size of its human population, Wyoming's cattle and sheep populations are huge. Furthermore, rangeland there covers a whopping 88 percent of the farmland.

CANADA

Nevada
page 106

COLORADO RIVER

ARKANSAS RIVER

Oklahoma
page 110

Arizona
page 104

New
Mexico
page 108

RED RIVER

Texas
page 112

RIO GRANDE

MEXICO

PACIFIC OCEAN

GULF OF MEXICO

Much of the Southwest belongs to the Great Basin, an arid region between the Rockies and the Pacific coastal ranges where water is scarce. The most important source of water in the Great Basin is the Colorado River, from which a great deal of drinking water is already being diverted to quench the thirst of people in southern California. Now fast-growing Arizona is building more pipeline to carry even more water from the Colorado. Meanwhile, the water table keeps dropping, creating deep cracks in the land.

Southwest

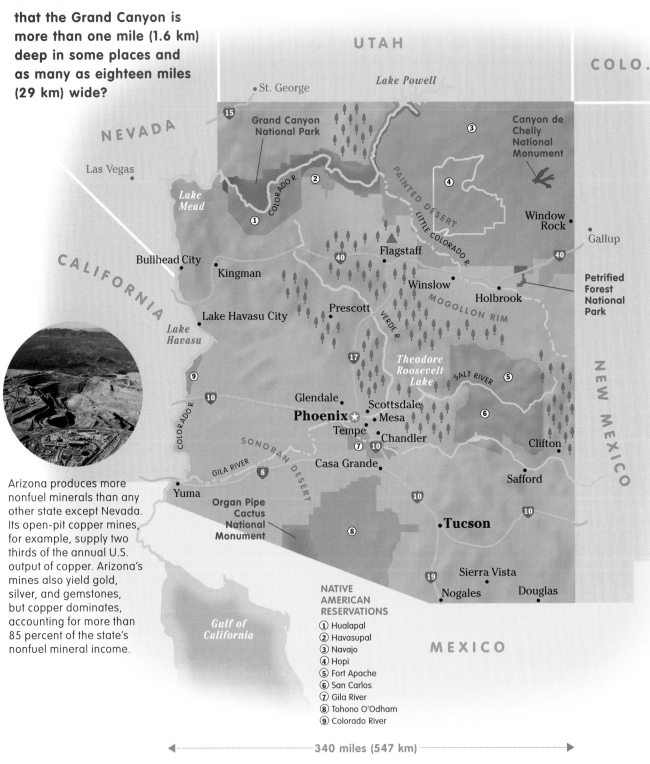

LEGEND

20 Interstate Highways   ★ State Capital   ▢ Native American Reservations   🌲 National Forests   ▪ National Parks and Refuges   ▲ Highest Point

| 0 | miles | 100 |
| 0 | kilometers | 161 |

DID YOU KNOW?

that the Grand Canyon is more than one mile (1.6 km) deep in some places and as many as eighteen miles (29 km) wide?

UTAH

COLO.

Lake Powell

• St. George

15

Grand Canyon National Park

NEVADA

3

Canyon de Chelly National Monument

Las Vegas •

COLORADO R.

2

PAINTED DESERT

4

LITTLE COLORADO R.

Window Rock •

• Gallup

Lake Mead

1

CALIFORNIA

Bullhead City •

Kingman •

40

Flagstaff

Winslow

MOGOLLON RIM

Holbrook

40

Petrified Forest National Park

Lake Havasu City •

Prescott

VERDE R.

Lake Havasu

17

Theodore Roosevelt Lake

SALT RIVER

5

9

10

Glendale

Scottsdale

6

Phoenix ★

• Mesa

Clifton •

COLORADO R.

Tempe

Chandler

7

10

NEW MEXICO

SONORAN DESERT

Casa Grande

Safford •

GILA RIVER

8

10

Yuma

Organ Pipe Cactus National Monument

Tucson

10

8

19

Sierra Vista

Nogales •

Douglas •

Gulf of California

MEXICO

Arizona produces more nonfuel minerals than any other state except Nevada. Its open-pit copper mines, for example, supply two thirds of the annual U.S. output of copper. Arizona's mines also yield gold, silver, and gemstones, but copper dominates, accounting for more than 85 percent of the state's nonfuel mineral income.

NATIVE AMERICAN RESERVATIONS

1. Hualapal
2. Havasupai
3. Navajo
4. Hopi
5. Fort Apache
6. San Carlos
7. Gila River
8. Tohono O'Odham
9. Colorado River

◄———————— 340 miles (547 km) ————————►

ABOUT ARIZONA

NICKNAME: Grand Canyon State

CAPITAL: Phoenix

STATEHOOD: February 14, 1912 (48th)

MOTTO: God enriches.

POPULATION: 5,307,331 (20th)

AREA: 114,006 sq. mi. (6th) (295,148 sq km)

HIGHEST POINT: 12,633 ft. (Humphreys Peak)

LOWEST POINT: 70 ft. (Colorado River)

FLOWER: Saguaro

TREE: Paloverde

BIRD: Cactus wren

FISH: Apache trout

Arizona

Arizona has always been known for its clean air and abundant sunshine. Yet until the 1960s, life in this desert state appealed mostly to people with breathing problems because the heat was so intense. With the advent of affordable air conditioning, however, many retired Americans also began to take advantage of the region's climate. Now, with manufacturing and construction jobs booming there, people of all ages are flocking to Arizona, which trails only Nevada as the nation's fastest-growing state.

Most of these newcomers have settled in the sprawling suburbs of Phoenix and Tucson, where four out of every five Arizonans live. However, the arrival of all these people has threatened—ironically—the very qualities of life that initially attracted them (and so many others) to the Sun Belt. More cars mean dirtier air, more new homes mean less natural scenery, and more people in general mean a greater strain on the state's natural resources, especially its water.

Arizona's most important source of water is the Colorado River, running through the 277-mile-long (446-kilometer -long) Grand Canyon. The canyon sits on the western edge of the scenic Colorado Plateau—a dry, high tableland cut by deep gorges and studded with mesas. A line of cliffs called the Mogollon Rim separates the Colorado Plateau from the Basin and Range system that covers southern and western Arizona. The "basins" of this system are the arid plains of the Sonoran Desert from which mountain "ranges" such as the Chiricahua rise occasionally, like islands from the sea.

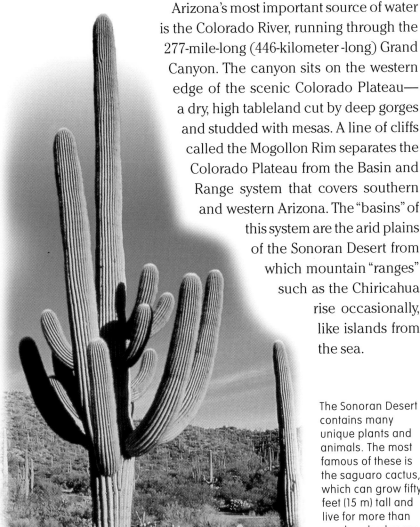

The Sonoran Desert contains many unique plants and animals. The most famous of these is the saguaro cactus, which can grow fifty feet (15 m) tall and live for more than one hundred years.

Although no longer a part of Mexico, Arizona continues to maintain strong ties to its southern neighbor. Because one in four Arizonans is Hispanic, Mexican influences abound. Mexican architecture, home furnishings, clothing, music, and food have all become important parts of the Arizona lifestyle.

BIG SANDY RIVER
LITTLE COLORADO R.
CHINLE WASH
SANTA MARIA R.
GILA RIVER
SAN PEDRO RIVER
BRAWLEY WASH

Mapmakers use dots and dashes to show rivers that dry up during part of the year. There are many such intermittent rivers in Arizona. Stretches of the Little Colorado, for example, flow only during winter and spring, when rains and melting snow provide sufficient water.

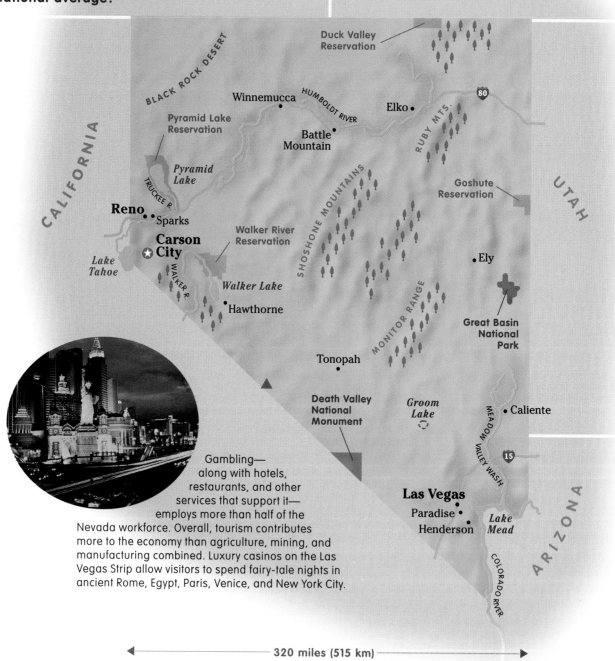

Interstate Highways · **State Capital** · **Native American Reservations** · **National Forests** · **National Parks and Refuges** · **Highest Point**

```
0          miles      100
0        kilometers    161
```

DID YOU KNOW?

that Nevada, with no waiting periods and many drive-through chapels, leads the nation in weddings with ten times the national average?

OREGON

IDAHO

Duck Valley Reservation

BLACK ROCK DESERT

Winnemucca

HUMBOLDT RIVER

Elko

80

Pyramid Lake Reservation

Battle Mountain

RUBY MTS.

CALIFORNIA

Pyramid Lake

TRUCKEE R.

Goshute Reservation

UTAH

Reno

Sparks

SHOSHONE MOUNTAINS

Carson City

Walker River Reservation

Ely

Lake Tahoe

WALKER R.

Walker Lake

MONITOR RANGE

Hawthorne

Great Basin National Park

Tonopah

Death Valley National Monument

Groom Lake

Caliente

MEADOW VALLEY WASH

15

Gambling— along with hotels, restaurants, and other services that support it— employs more than half of the Nevada workforce. Overall, tourism contributes more to the economy than agriculture, mining, and manufacturing combined. Luxury casinos on the Las Vegas Strip allow visitors to spend fairy-tale nights in ancient Rome, Egypt, Paris, Venice, and New York City.

Las Vegas

Paradise

Henderson

Lake Mead

ARIZONA

COLORADO RIVER

◄-------- 320 miles (515 km) --------►

ABOUT NEVADA

NICKNAME: Silver State

CAPITAL: Carson City

STATEHOOD: October 31, 1864 (36th)

MOTTO: All for our country.

POPULATION: 2,106,074 (35th)

AREA: 110,567 sq. mi. (7th)
(286,245 sq km)

HIGHEST POINT: 13,140 ft. (Boundary Peak)

LOWEST POINT: 479 ft. (Colorado River)

FLOWER: Sagebrush

TREE: Single-leaf piñon, bristlecone pine

BIRD: Mountain bluebird

FISH: Lahontan cutthroat trout

Nevada

Because of its excessively dry climate and barren landscape, Nevada was one of the last U.S. territories to be explored and settled. Nineteenth-century gold and silver strikes lured prospectors—and Nevada still leads the nation in gold and silver mining—but those prospectors didn't stay long. During the Great Depression, Nevada attracted some attention with laws that made marriage and divorce much easier, yet it was legalized gambling, enacted in 1931, that assured the state's future prosperity.

Although Nevada retains many rugged frontier qualities, casino money has transformed both Las Vegas and Reno into sophisticated metropolitan areas housing more than 80 percent of the state's population. With the exception of the southern desert, the rest of the state belongs to what residents call the "cow counties," where cattle and sheep graze on leased public land before being shipped to California or the Midwest for fattening. The lack of water, of course, limits most other types of agriculture.

In fact, with just nine inches (23 cm) of precipitation per year, Nevada is the driest state. Except for a small spur of the Sierra Nevada near Lake Tahoe, most of Nevada belongs to the arid Great Basin. The water that makes Las Vegas possible comes primarily from Lake Mead, the largest U.S. reservoir, which stretches for 115 miles (185 km) behind the Hoover Dam on the Colorado River.

Nevada's clear skies and open desert terrain provide ideal conditions for testing military aircraft. Over the years, many mysterious planes have been tested at Area 51, a top-secret air force base near Groom Lake. Often these planes are mistaken for UFOs. As a result, Route 375, which runs past Groom Lake, has been nicknamed the Extraterrestrial Highway.

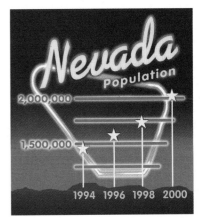

Nevada is the nation's fastest-growing state. Since 1980, its population has more than doubled. Nearly all that growth has come within existing metropolitan areas, especially the suburbs of Las Vegas.

Although Nevada averages nine inches (23 cm) of precipitation per year statewide, less than four inches (10 cm) of rain falls on the parched southern Nevada desert, where Death Valley National Monument is located.

107

LEGEND

20 Interstate Highways	State Capital	Native American Reservations	National Forests	National Parks and Refuges	Highest Point	0 miles 100	0 kilometers 161

Since the 1940s, the Los Alamos National Laboratory has made New Mexico a center for scientific research. Los Alamos and other federal facilities, including the Sandia National Laboratories in Albuquerque, attract highly educated workers, often from outside the state.

UTAH

COLORADO

OKLA.

Durango

Farmington ①
SAN JUAN RIVER

②

Raton

DID YOU KNOW?

that at Four Corners on the Navajo Reservation you can lie down in four states at the same time?

22

Taos

③

SANGRE DE CRISTO MTS.

25

④
Los Alamos ⑤ ⑥ ⑦
⑧
Santa Fe

RIO PUERCO

⑨
⑩ ⑨
⑩ ⑪ ⑫ ⑬

Las Vegas

Conchas Lake
CANADIAN R.

Gallup

40

RIO GRANDE

⑭
Rio Rancho
Albuquerque

Tucumcari

⑮
⑳ ⑰ ⑭ ⑯
⑲ 40

TEXAS

⑭

Clovis

MAJOR NATIVE AMERICAN RESERVATIONS

① Ute Mountain
② Jicarilla Apache
③ Taos
④ Santa Clara
⑤ San Ildefonso
⑥ Pojaoque
⑦ Nambe
⑧ Tesuque
⑨ Jemez
⑩ Zia
⑪ Santa Ana
⑫ Santo Domingo
⑬ San Filipe
⑭ Laguna
⑮ Cañoncito
⑯ Isleta
⑰ Acoma
⑱ Alamo Navajo
⑲ Ramah Navajo
⑳ Zuni
㉑ Mescalero
㉒ Navajo

⑱
Socorro

25

Portales

GILA RIVER

PECOS RIVER

Elephant Butte Reservoir
• Truth or Consequences

Roswell

Silver City

㉑
Alamogordo

Hobbs

Carlsbad

Las Cruces
White Sands National Monument

Carlsbad Caverns National Park

10 Deming
10

• El Paso

MEXICO

◄--------- 352 miles (566 km) ---------►

ABOUT NEW MEXICO

NICKNAME: Land of Enchantment	**POPULATION:** 1,829,146 (36th)	**FLOWER:** Yucca
CAPITAL: Santa Fe	**AREA:** 121,598 sq. mi. (5th)	**TREE:** Piñon
STATEHOOD: January 6, 1912 (47th)	(314,803 sq km)	**BIRD:** Roadrunner
MOTTO: It grows as it goes.	**HIGHEST POINT:** 13,161 ft. (Wheeler Peak)	**FISH:** Rio Grande cutthroat trout
	LOWEST POINT: 2,842 ft. (Red Bluff Reservoir)	

New Mexico

For many years, New Mexico has attracted top artists from all over the world. Painters, notably Georgia O'Keeffe, came to record the state's unique physical beauty. Writers, on the other hand, have generally been more interested in observing New Mexico's extraordinary cultural diversity. With a population that's 42 percent Hispanic (the highest percentage of any state) and 9 percent Native American (the second highest percentage), New Mexico is an ongoing experiment. The purpose of this experiment? To find out how people of radically different backgrounds can live together while still maintaining their separate cultural identities.

Although art galleries have prospered in Santa Fe and Taos, most New Mexicans depend on farming, ranching, and mining for their livelihoods. New Mexico, for example, ranks third in copper production, sixth in uranium, and enjoys large reserves of oil, coal, and natural gas. In 1999, despite some local opposition, the nation's first permanent nuclear waste disposal site opened in the desert east of Carlsbad, accepting radioactive waste from Los Alamos and other nuclear weapons laboratories.

New Mexico's eastern third, a part of the Great Plains, is often called Little Texas because its cattle ranches, oil fields, and military bases remind people of the state next door. Farther west, the fertile Rio Grande Valley runs through the southern Rockies. The rest of the state belongs to the high Colorado Plateau in the northwest and a Basin and Range system in the south.

The Navajo of New Mexico are famous for their blankets, the Zuni for their turquoise-and-silver jewelry, and the Pueblo for their pots. Pueblo pottery is typically painted with geometric designs that identify the potter's village.

Humorist Will Rogers once called the enormous Carlsbad Caverns "the Grand Canyon with a roof on it." From late spring through fall, three hundred thousand Mexican free-tailed bats depart nightly at dusk to hunt for insects. People have compared this swarm to a column of smoke rising from the cave entrance.

From the desert basins of southern New Mexico, the land rises steadily as one moves north, climbing ten thousand feet (3,000 m) to the snowy Sangre de Cristo Mountains north of Taos.

LEGEND

🛣 20 Interstate Highways	✪ State Capital	⬜ Native American Reservations	🌲 National Forests	⬛ National Parks and Refuges	🌾 Grasslands	▲ Highest Point	0 miles 100	0 kilometers 161

Pump It Up

Wells are a familiar sight in Oklahoma. In fact, eighteen wells once pumped oil from beneath the grounds of the state capitol. Although nearly every county in Oklahoma has oil and natural gas, the most important fields are found near Tulsa, the center of the state's petroleum industry.

KANSAS

COL.

N.M.

MISSOURI

ARKANSAS

TEXAS

Wichita

Salt Plains National Wildlife Refuge

Osage Reservation

Guymon • Optima Lake

Alva

SALT FORK RIVER

Ponca City

Bartlesville

Miami

Woodward

Great Salt Plains Lake

Enid

CIMARRON RIVER

Lake of the Cherokees

Canton Lake

Stillwater

Tulsa •

Broken Arrow

CANADIAN R.

35

Edmond

Midwest City

Muskogee

ARKANSAS R.

Fort Smith

DID YOU KNOW?

that Oklahoma averages fifty tornadoes a year, with the most coming in April and May?

Elk City

40

Oklahoma City ✪

Shawnee

44

Eufaula Lake

40

Robert S. Kerr Lake

Anadarko

Norman

WICHITA MTS.

WASHITA RIVER

Ada

McAlester

OUACHITA MTS.

Altus

Lawton

35

Broken Bow Lake

44

Duncan

Ardmore

Lake Texoma

Idabel

RED RIVER

Fort Worth   Dallas

◄———————— 464 miles (747 km) ————————►

ABOUT OKLAHOMA

NICKNAME: Sooner State	**POPULATION:** 3,460,097 (28th)	**FLOWER:** Mistletoe
CAPITAL: Oklahoma City	**AREA:** 69,903 sq. mi. (20th)	**TREE:** Redbud
STATEHOOD: November 16, 1907 (46th)	(180,971 sq km)	**BIRD:** Scissor-tailed flycatcher
MOTTO: Labor conquers all.	**HIGHEST POINT:** 4,973 ft. (Black Mesa)	**FISH:** White bass
	LOWEST POINT: 289 ft. (Little River)	

Oklahoma

The people who live along the Red River in southern Oklahoma call their region Little Dixie because it reminds them of the Deep South, where their great-great-grandfathers farmed before moving west. Similarly, the wheat fields of northern Oklahoma show the influence of the transplanted Kansans who first tilled the soil there. However, from the Ouachita Mountains to the Panhandle, the rest of Oklahoma is truly cowboy country, and the state prides itself on its colorful western heritage.

For a long time, both the cowboys and the Native Americans in Oklahoma struggled. During the nineteenth century, Oklahoma was called the Indian Territory because the federal government had relocated so many Native Americans there. The terrain was so barren that no one thought whites would ever want to live there. Even during the twentieth century, the prolonged drought of the Dust Bowl years forced hundreds of thousands of Oklahomans to leave the state.

Yet today the descendants of Oklahoma's cowboys and Native Americans are flourishing. Improved soil conservation has reclaimed so much farmland that Oklahoma currently ranks fourth in wheat production. It also ranks third in beef cattle, the state's leading agricultural product. Even bigger money comes from oil and natural gas.

Overall, Oklahoma is a jumble of environments: The northeastern corner, for example, sits on the edge of the hilly, cool Ozark Plateau. The High Plains climate on the Panhandle, however, is much hotter and drier.

After California, Oklahoma has more Native American residents than any other state—about 270,000, or 7.9 percent of the population. Yet there are few reservations in Oklahoma because the Cherokee and other Native American nations have become so well integrated. In 1985, for example, the Cherokee Nation took the nontraditional step of electing its first female chief, Wilma Mankiller (pictured above).

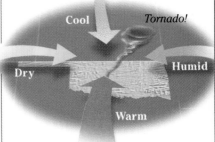

Oklahoma has extremely varied microclimates because it occupies two weather transition zones: from north to south as well as from east to west. At any given time, cool northern, warm southern, dry western, or humid eastern air may dominate. However, when two or more of these air masses meet, the result can be a blizzard, a thunderstorm, or even a tornado.

The humid Red River Valley defines Oklahoma's southern border with Texas. The farmers there grow cotton, peanuts, and other crops that immigrants from the South brought with them during the nineteenth century.

LEGEND

Interstate Highways	State Capital	National Parks and Refuges	National Forests	Marshes	Grasslands	Highest Point	0 miles 100 / 0 kilometers 161

DID YOU KNOW?

that Austin is home to the largest urban bat colony in the United States?

CANADIAN RIVER

Oklahoma City

O K L A H O M A

N E W   M E X I C O

Amarillo

Clovis

LLANO ESTACADO

RED RIVER

Wichita Falls

Sherman

A R K.

Texarkana

Wright Patman Lake

Lubbock

Guadalupe Mountains National Park

Abilene

Fort Worth

Dallas

Arlington

Longview

Shreveport

Tyler

L O U I S.

TRINITY RIVER

El Paso

Midland

Odessa

San Angelo

COLORADO RIVER

Waco

BRAZOS RIVER

SABINE RIVER

Toledo Bend Reservoir

PECOS RIVER

DAVIS MTS.

EDWARDS PLATEAU

Sam Rayburn Reservoir

Austin ☆

Houston

Beaumont

Big Bend National Park

Del Rio

San Antonio

Pasadena

Galveston

M E X I C O

NUECES RIVER

RIO GRANDE

Victoria

G U L F   O F   M E X I C O

Laredo

Corpus Christi

Padre Island National Seashore

To reduce its dependence on oil, the Texas economy has become more diversified. Computer firms in Austin's Silicon Hills have created many new jobs, while others have come from an older industry: cattle ranching. The King Ranch south of Corpus Christi, the largest ranch in the United States, covers 825,000 acres (334,000 ha), which is about the size of Rhode Island.

801 miles (1,289 km)

ABOUT TEXAS

NICKNAME: Lone Star State

CAPITAL: Austin

STATEHOOD: December 29, 1845 (28th)

MOTTO: Friendship.

POPULATION: 21,325,018 (2nd)

AREA: 268,601 sq. mi. (2nd)
(695,376 sq km)

HIGHEST POINT: 8,749 ft. (Guadalupe Peak)

LOWEST POINT: Sea level (Gulf of Mexico)

FLOWER: Bluebonnet

TREE: Pecan

BIRD: Mockingbird

FISH: Guadalupe bass

Texas

When Texas joined the Union in 1845, Congress gave it the right to divide itself into five states of more manageable size. Instead, Texas has remained huge—the second largest state, the second most populous, and among the wealthiest. Over the years, Texans have used their valuable natural resources, particularly oil, to fund the growth of profitable manufacturing industries, such as chemical production.

Houston, the center of the U.S. petroleum industry and one of the nation's busiest ports, sits on the Gulf Coastal Plain, which covers the state's eastern third. This highly industrialized and densely populated region includes Texas's best farmland and its most productive oil fields.

A line drawn from Fort Worth to San Antonio would separate the moist coastal plain from the dry, treeless hill country, where cattle ranching still dominates. Ranching is also the dominant industry on the High Plains of the Panhandle—where, it's said, the cowboy spirit endures. Farther south, in the Rio Grande Valley, an eleven-month growing season allows farmers to raise winter vegetables and some citrus fruit.

The Rio Grande Valley is also known for its high concentration of Mexican Americans. Hispanics account for nearly a third of Texas's population, making them an important political force in cities such as El Paso and San Antonio. In fact, census projections suggest that Texas will one day have a Hispanic majority.

Austin calls itself the Live Music Capital of the World because of the many nightclubs lining downtown Sixth Street. The diverse styles heard there include blues, country, jazz, swing, and Tejano.

— Interstate Highways and State Roads

Texas has more streets and highways than any other state. Its 294,833 total miles (474,386 km) are nearly twice that of second-place California. The state's annual roadway maintenance budget, which doesn't include money spent by towns or counties, is more than eight hundred million dollars, and its construction budget is nearly two billion dollars.

Texas boasts more than five thousand species of wildflowers. Although bluebonnet, pink evening primrose, and Indian paintbrush grow statewide, most varieties are confined to a particular region.

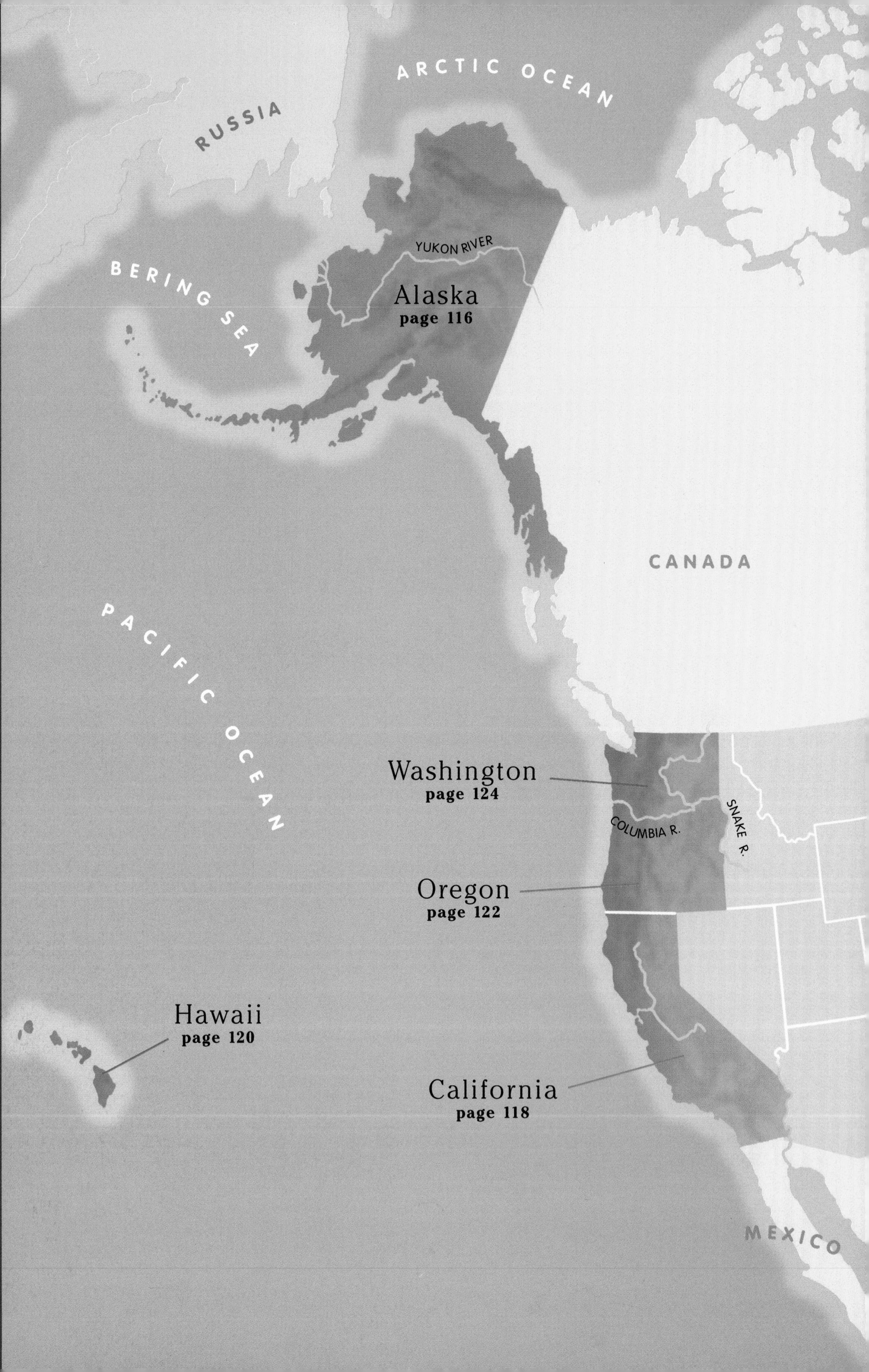

ARCTIC OCEAN

RUSSIA

CANADA

BERING SEA

YUKON RIVER

Alaska
page 116

PACIFIC OCEAN

Washington
page 124

COLUMBIA R.

SNAKE R.

Oregon
page 122

Hawaii
page 120

California
page 118

MEXICO

T he Coast Ranges of California, Oregon, and Washington form a line along which the Pacific and North American plates (part of the earth's crust) crunch past one another. Earthquakes, with which most Californians are familiar, are one symptom of this stress. Another is volcanic activity, such as the eruption of Mount St. Helens in 1980. The Aleutian Islands of Alaska also sit on this Ring of Fire, the name given to the edge of the Pacific Plate along which most of the earth's active volcanoes are located.

Pacific

The Trans-Alaska Pipeline carries oil from Prudhoe Bay, where the coast is frozen eight months a year, to the ice-free port of Valdez eight hundred miles (1,300 km) away. Terrain permitting, the four-foot-wide (one-meter-wide) pipeline is buried. However, across the permanently frozen Arctic tundra, it's typically raised on supports that allow migrating caribou to pass underneath.

ARCTIC OCEAN

Barrow

Prudhoe Bay

Chukchi Sea

NORTH SLOPE

COLVILLE RIVER

BROOKS RANGE

NOATAK RIVER

⑦

Kotzebue

⑧

PORCUPINE R.

RUSSIA

Bering Strait

Nome

KOYUKUK R.

YUKON RIVER

College   Fairbanks

C A N A D A

KUSKOKWIM MTS.

YUKON RIVER

TANANA RIVER

BERING SEA

KUSKOKWIM RIVER

ALASKA RANGE

⑥

WRANGELL MTS.

Bethel

Anchorage

⑤   Valdez

Kenai

②   Whitehorse

③

Cordova

Prince William Sound

④

Skagway

①

DID YOU KNOW?

that because the Matanuska Valley north of Anchorage gets twenty hours of sunlight during summer, cabbages there grow to nearly one hundred pounds (45 kg)?

Kodiak

Kodiak Island

Juneau ★

Gulf of Alaska

Sitka

Alexander Archipelago

ALEUTIAN RANGE

Cold Bay

Ketchikan

NATIONAL PARKS

① Glacier Bay
② Wrangell–St. Elias
③ Kenai Fjords
④ Katmai
⑤ Lake Clark
⑥ Denali
⑦ Gates of the Arctic
⑧ Kobuk Valley

Unalaska

Aleutian Islands

PACIFIC OCEAN

◄──────── 2,400 miles (3,862 km) ────────►

ABOUT ALASKA

NICKNAME: Last Frontier

CAPITAL: Juneau

STATEHOOD: January 3, 1959 (49th)

MOTTO: North to the future.

POPULATION: 619,500 (48th)

AREA: 656,424 sq. mi. (1st)
(1,699,404 sq km)

HIGHEST POINT: 20,320 ft. (Mount McKinley)

LOWEST POINT: Sea level (Pacific Ocean)

FLOWER: Forget-me-not

TREE: Sitka spruce

BIRD: Willow ptarmigan

FISH: King salmon

Alaska

Alaska can be a hard place to live because of the cold climate and rough terrain. In January, for example, the temperature in Fairbanks rarely rises above 0°F (-18°C), and even during the summer months, mountain ranges and ice fields make ground-level travel difficult, as do the great distances involved.

Alaskans have made up for this isolation by using satellite telephones and the Internet to connect to the outside world. Among the most ardent users of these new technologies are the native people who make up 16 percent of the population. Even so, many Aleuts and Inuit still live off the land, hunting and fishing as their ancestors did.

The dominant physical feature of the Alaskan Panhandle is the Inside Passage, a sheltered waterway stretching from Skagway to Seattle, Washington. Through its channels runs the Alaska Marine Highway, a state-operated ferry system that services towns with little or no road access. Far more remote are the fogbound Aleutian Islands, jutting eleven hundred miles (1,800 km) into the North Pacific.

Inland, north of the Alaska Range, sits the Yukon Plateau, beyond which few Alaskans live. From the crest of the little-explored Brooks Range, the land slopes down to the Arctic Coastal Plain, where immense oil fields were discovered in 1968. Currently, oil revenues fund about 85 percent of the state budget, but Alaskans have also had to live with oil's environmental consequences, such as the 1989 *Exxon Valdez* spill that polluted Prince William Sound.

In rugged Alaska, the family "car" is often a small airplane. One out of every fifty-eight Alaskans has a license to fly, which is six times the national average. Even where there are roads, snowmobiles often take the place of cars in winter.

Alaska, the largest state, accounts for one sixth of the nation's total area. If you superimposed a map of Alaska on a map of the continental United States, Alaska would stretch all the way from Savannah, Georgia, to Los Angeles and reach as far north as the Canadian border.

The towering peaks of the Alaska Range dominate the southern half of the state. These include Mount McKinley, the highest point in North America. Of the twenty tallest U.S. mountains, seventeen are in Alaska.

OREGON

Redwood National Park

KLAMATH RIVER

KLAMATH MTS.

CASCADE MTS.

Goose Lake

① Eureka

⑤

Lassen Volcanic National Park

Shasta Lake

EEL RIVER

SACRAMENTO R.

Redding

② Chico

Reno

In California's fertile Central Valley, farmers grow more than 350 varieties of fruits and vegetables. When processed, these crops make up about 40 percent of the nation's canned and frozen produce. Super-markets can sell California produce cheaply because much of it is picked by migrant workers who work under difficult conditions for little pay.

Clear Lake

COAST RANGES

Santa Rosa

⑤⑤⑤

Sacramento ★

80

Lake Tahoe

80

NEVADA

Yosemite National Park

Mono Lake

MAJOR NATIVE AMERICAN RESERVATIONS

① Hoopa Valley
② Round Valley
③ Tule River
④ Aqua Caliente

Berkeley

80

San Francisco

⑤

Stockton

Oakland

Modesto

Sunnyvale

San Jose

Merced

Santa Cruz

SAN JOAQUIN R.

Kings Canyon National Park

Death Valley National Park

SIERRA NEVADA

Salinas

Fresno

Monterey

SALINAS RIVER

COAST RANGES

⑤

Sequoia National Park

③

Las Vegas

San Luis Obispo

Bakersfield

MOJAVE DESERT

15

ARIZONA

COLORADO RIVER

Barstow

40

Santa Barbara

15

Joshua Tree National Park

DID YOU KNOW?

that the highest (Mount Whitney) and the lowest (Death Valley) points in the continental United States are only sixty miles (97 km) apart?

PACIFIC OCEAN

Los Angeles

Pasadena

San Bernardino

Anaheim

Riverside

Long Beach

Santa Ana

④

Channel Islands National Park

Channel Islands

San Diego

⑤ 15

10

Salton Sea

8

Escondido

Chula Vista

Tijuana

MEXICO

|← 350 miles (563 km) →|

ABOUT CALIFORNIA

NICKNAME: Golden State	POPULATION: 33,145,121 (1st)	FLOWER: Golden poppy
CAPITAL: Sacramento	AREA: 163,707 sq. mi. (3rd)	TREE: California redwood
STATEHOOD: September 9, 1850 (31st)	(423,818 sq km)	BIRD: California valley quail
MOTTO: Eureka!	HIGHEST POINT: 14,494 ft. (Mount Whitney)	FISH: California golden trout
	LOWEST POINT: -282 ft. (Death Valley)	

California

CALIFORNIA REPUBLIC

A century ago, immigrants from all over the world flocked to New York City to earn their fortunes. Since World War II, however, even New Yorkers have gone to California to make their dreams come true—and not just out-of-work actors. Today, it's impossible to overstate California's economic, political, and cultural importance. The state ranks first in both manufactured goods and farm income, and without California's votes it's difficult to win a presidential election. Cultural trends, too, now move from west to east: Two recent examples are organic foods and eastern religion (no doubt influenced by the many Asian Americans living in California). Overall, nearly one in eight Americans is a Californian, including half of all Mexican Americans and two fifths of all Asian Americans, many of whom are recent immigrants.

Although southern California is famous for its beaches, most of it sits on the Mojave Desert. As a result, the region has 50 percent of the state's population but only 2 percent of its water. That's why a complex system of dams and aqueducts has been built to divert water from elsewhere, principally the Colorado River.

North of the fertile Central Valley, which runs between the Coast Ranges and the Sierra Nevada, the Klamath and Cascade mountains rise above dense stands of timber. Except in the desert south, California has two seasons: a dry one from spring to fall and a rainy one the rest of the year.

Alice Waters, the founder of Berkeley's Chez Panisse restaurant, began a trend in cooking that has since come to be known as California cuisine. Her cooking emphasizes the freshest ingredients, usually grown organically on small local farms, and borrows freely from California's many immigrant cuisines, especially Asian and Mexican.

In earthquake-prone California, two of the plates that make up the earth's crust come together. The line along which they meet is called the San Andreas Fault. As the Pacific Plate creeps northwestward, it pushes against the North American Plate, causing pressure to build. From time to time, this pressure is released as an earthquake.

California's largest cities are all located at gaps in the Coast Ranges. Elsewhere, these mountains rise so abruptly from the Pacific that towns have no room to grow. There's barely enough room for State Route 1, which is often closed by mud slides.

LEGEND

⭐ State Capital

⬛ National Parks and Refuges

🔺 Highest Point

0 ——— miles ——— 100
0 ——— kilometers ——— 161

DID YOU KNOW?

that despite the tropical climate, snow falls on Hawaii's tallest mountains?

Kauai

Kapaa
Kekaha • Lihue
Puuwai •

Niihau

Oahu

Pearl City • Kaneohe
Waipahu • • Kailua
Honolulu ⭐
Pearl Harbor

Molokai

Kaunakakai •

Maui

Wailuku
Lanai City • • Kahului
Kihei •

Lanai

Haleakala National Park

Kahoolawe

PACIFIC OCEAN

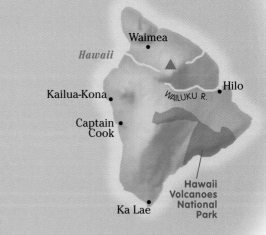

Waimea •
Hawaii

Kailua-Kona •
WAILUKU R.
Hilo •

Captain Cook •

Hawaii Volcanoes National Park

Ka Lae •

Hawaii leads the nation in raising bananas, papayas, guavas, macadamia nuts, and coffee, as well as pineapples, the state's most famous crop. Each year, the pineapple harvest brings in about one hundred million dollars.

←————— 353 miles (568 km) —————→

ABOUT HAWAII

NICKNAME: Aloha State

CAPITAL: Honolulu

STATEHOOD: August 21, 1959 (50th)

MOTTO: The life of the land is perpetuated in righteousness.

POPULATION: 1,185,497 (42nd)

AREA: 10,932 sq. mi. (43rd) (28,302 sq km)

HIGHEST POINT: 13,796 ft. (Mauna Kea)

LOWEST POINT: Sea level (Pacific Ocean)

FLOWER: Yellow hibiscus

TREE: Kukui (candlenut)

BIRD: Nene (Hawaiian goose)

Hawaii

The familiar Hawaiian islands are, in fact, the eastern end of a sixteen-hundred-mile (twenty-six-hundred-kilometer) chain stretching from the Big Island of Hawaii northwest to tiny Kure Atoll. Nearly all Hawaiians live on the eight major islands, which are the cone-shaped tops of gigantic ocean volcanoes. Of these people, 21 percent are descendants of the Polynesians who originally settled Hawaii. The rest are 33 percent white, 20 percent Japanese, 10 percent Filipino, 3 percent Chinese, and 3 percent black, giving Hawaii the most diverse ethnic mix of any state.

Even so, Hawaii's population is dwarfed each year by the seven million tourists who bring with them ten billion dollars, by far the state's largest source of income. The next largest revenue producer is the federal government. Military bases such as Pearl Harbor house so many soldiers and sailors that military personnel and their families make up nearly one tenth of the state's population.

The most crowded island is Oahu, where about three in four Hawaiians live. The largest island is agricultural Hawaii. Kauai's lush valleys, Maui's wide beaches, and Lanai's seclusion are particularly popular with tourists, while Molokai and Niihau have especially high concentrations of native Hawaiians. On the tiny, privately owned island of Niihau, several hundred pure-blood Hawaiians raise livestock, speak their traditional language, and otherwise struggle to keep native traditions alive. Public access to Niihau is strictly limited, and no one at all is allowed on Kahoolawe, which until recently was a bombing range.

"Shaka, Brah"

Among young people in Hawaii, the "shaka" sign is the universal greeting. Given with the thumb pointing up and the pinkie pointing out, it means both "hello" and "peace"—and, more generally— "good vibes." It's often accompanied by the phrase "Shaka, Brah." (*Brah* is pidgin English for "brother.")

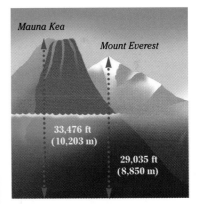

Mauna Kea

Mount Everest

33,476 ft
(10,203 m)

29,035 ft
(8,850 m)

The state's highest point, Mauna Kea on the Big Island of Hawaii, rises 13,796 feet (4,205 m) above sea level. It also extends nearly 20,000 feet (6,000 m) down to the bottom of the Hawaiian Trough. If you count this submerged base, Mauna Kea becomes the tallest mountain in the world, topping even Mount Everest.

The white sand that covers most Hawaiian beaches is made of tiny shell and coral fragments pulverized by the pounding surf. Some beaches, however, have black sand made of crushed obsidian, which is also called volcanic glass.

121

LEGEND

 Interstate Highways

State Capital

Native American Reservations

National Forests

National Parks and Refuges

Highest Point

| 0 | miles | 100 |
| 0 | kilometers | 161 |

Although the timber industry no longer dominates the state economy, it remains important to the way that Oregonians view themselves. Each July, for example, the Albany Timber Carnival sponsors popular competitions in log chopping, sawing, ax throwing, and birling (log rolling in water).

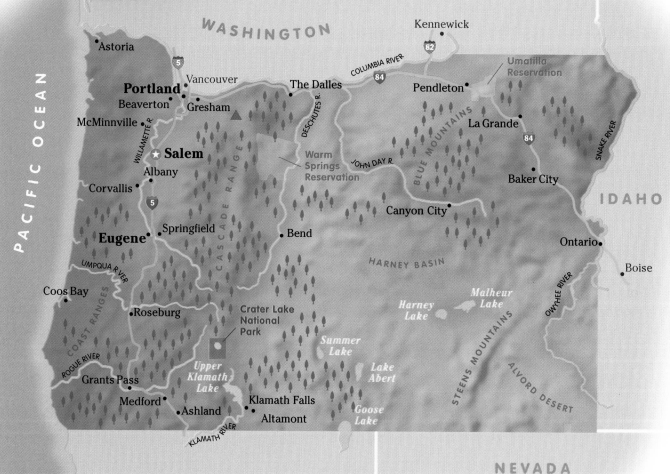

DID YOU KNOW?

that Oregon, a national leader in ecological legislation, passed the nation's first bottle-return law in 1971?

395 miles (636 km)

ABOUT OREGON

NICKNAME: Beaver State

CAPITAL: Salem

STATEHOOD: February 14, 1859 (33rd)

MOTTO: She flies with her own wings.

POPULATION: 3,316,154 (28th)

AREA: 98,386 sq. mi. (9th) (254,710 sq km)

HIGHEST POINT: 11,239 ft. (Mount Hood)

LOWEST POINT: Sea level (Pacific Ocean)

FLOWER: Oregon grape

TREE: Douglas fir

BIRD: Western meadowlark

FISH: Chinook salmon

Oregon

STATE OF OREGON
1859

No one doubts that Oregonians love the outdoors. Excluding the state's passion for wrestling, bicycling and long-distance running are its most high-profile sports. Yet Oregon is also the nation's leading timber state, and until recently most Oregonians worked for timber-related companies. During the 1990s, though, they had to make hard choices between their jobs and the environment.

Some choices were made for them. To protect the habitat of the endangered northern spotted owl, the federal government severely restricted logging in public forests, which contain about half of Oregon's timber. In response, the state reduced its dependence on forestry by promoting high-tech industries like those in neighboring Washington and California.

Recent immigrants to Oregon say that they value the state's high quality of life, particularly its clean air and water, outdoor lifestyle, and many open spaces. In fact, outside the Willamette River Valley, Oregon is quite sparsely settled. The rainy, foggy, populated Oregon that most people picture in their minds exists only west of the Cascades. The rest of the state sits mostly on the dry, barren Columbia Plateau. Geologists call the land south of the Blue Mountains the High Lava Plains because it was once covered with lava from the volcano that erupted to form Crater Lake. To most people, though, this Utah-like landscape is simply the Oregon Desert.

Bicycle-friendly Portland has recently become even more so. In 1994, a community-based environmental group interested in reducing auto pollution began leaving free bicycles around the city for anyone to use. Riders are merely asked to return the bikes, painted a distinctive yellow, to a main street after each trip.

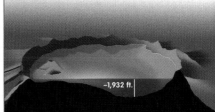

-1,932 ft.

Nearly eight thousand years ago, a volcano erupted in southern Oregon. The explosion blew off the mountain's peak, leaving behind a crater that has since filled with rainwater and snowmelt. Intensely blue Crater Lake is, at 1,932 feet (589 m), the deepest lake in the United States and the seventh deepest in the world.

Most Oregonians live in the fertile Willamette River Valley, running south from the Columbia River between the Coast Range and the Cascades. Many farms there grow flowering bulbs and plants such as tulips and the irises pictured at left.

123

LEGEND

Interstate Highways	State Capital	Native American Reservations
National Forests	National Parks and Refuges	Highest Point

0 — miles — 100
0 — kilometers — 161

DID YOU KNOW?

that the San Juan Islands in Puget Sound increase from 428 to 743 islands between high and low tides?

CANADA

Vancouver
Point Roberts
North Cascades National Park
Bellingham
Strait of San Juan de Fuca
San Juan Islands
Puget Sound
SKAGIT RIVER
Colville Reservation
KETTLE RIVER RANGE
COLUMBIA RIVER
Spokane Reservation
Port Angeles
5
Everett
CASCADE RANGE
Lake Chelan
WENATCHEE MTS.
Banks Lake
Grand Coulee
SPOKANE RIVER
Olympic National Park
OLYMPIC MTS.
Seattle
Bellevue
Federal Way
Wenatchee
Spokane
IDAHO
Quinault Reservation
COAST RANGES
Aberdeen
90
Tacoma
Olympia
Mount Rainier National Park
Ellensburg
Ephrata
Moses Lake
Potholes Reservoir
90
Centralia
Yakima
COLUMBIA RIVER
SNAKE RIVER
5
Longview Kelso
Richland
Kennewick
Mt. St. Helens National Volcanic Monument
Vancouver
YAKIMA RIVER
Yakima Reservation
82
Walla Walla
PACIFIC OCEAN
Portland
OREGON

Dams on the Snake and Columbia rivers produce about one third of all U.S. hydroelectric power. The most impressive is the Grand Coulee Dam, the nation's largest concrete structure. Many Washington businesses depend on its cheap renewable energy, such as the Reynolds Metals aluminum-smelting plant in Longview.

◄———— 360 miles (579 km) ————►

ABOUT WASHINGTON

NICKNAME: Evergreen State
CAPITAL: Olympia
STATEHOOD: November 11, 1889 (42nd)
MOTTO: By and by.

POPULATION: 5,756,361 (15th)
AREA: 71,302 sq. mi. (18th)
(184,592 sq km)
HIGHEST POINT: 14,410 ft. (Mount Rainier)
LOWEST POINT: Sea level (Pacific Ocean)

FLOWER: Coast rhododendron
TREE: Western hemlock
BIRD: Willow goldfinch
FISH: Steelhead trout

Washington

Besides the rain, what's not to like about Washington? From the snowcapped mountains to the islands of Puget Sound, the scenery is spectacular, and the state's economy is equally breathtaking. Perhaps that's why Seattle has become one of the nation's most desirable and fastest-growing cities.

About two thirds of the state's population lives on the shores of Puget Sound, where shipbuilding used to be the leading industry. Now it's computers. Boasting more than two thousand software companies, notably Microsoft, the Puget Sound basin has come to rival California's Silicon Valley as the nation's leading high-tech, high-wage center.

Elsewhere in western Washington, forestry companies harvest the abundant timber growing on the western slopes of the Olympic and Cascade mountains. That's where most of the rain falls, as much as two hundred inches (500 cm) per year. All that moisture nourishes a unique temperate rain forest thickly carpeted with ferns and mosses.

Yet just a few miles over the Cascades in eastern Washington, the Columbia Plateau is so dry that dams are needed to irrigate the fields. With enough water, though, the rich volcanic soil of the Columbia Plateau is well suited to agriculture. Among the most valuable crops grown there are apples, cherries, asparagus, raspberries, and wine grapes. The warm days, cool nights, and sandy soil of the Columbia River basin resemble the vineyard conditions in France, making for excellent grape growing.

As well as skiing, sailing, and mountain climbing, Washingtonians are particularly fond of wildlife watching. The ferry that carries commuters from the San Juan Islands to Seattle also provides the occasional opportunity to view the orcas, minke whales, and seals that live in Puget Sound.

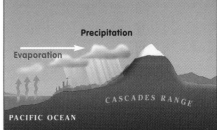

Why is western Washington so wet and eastern Washington so dry? Because the height of the Cascades forces clouds to drop their moisture before passing over. That's why the Olympic Peninsula receives 125 inches (318 cm) of precipitation per year and Richland on the Columbia River only 7 inches (18 cm).

Most of the high peaks in the Cascades are dormant volcanoes, yet every so often one becomes active. On May 18, 1980, long-dormant Mount St. Helens erupted, blanketing most of the Northwest with volcanic ash.

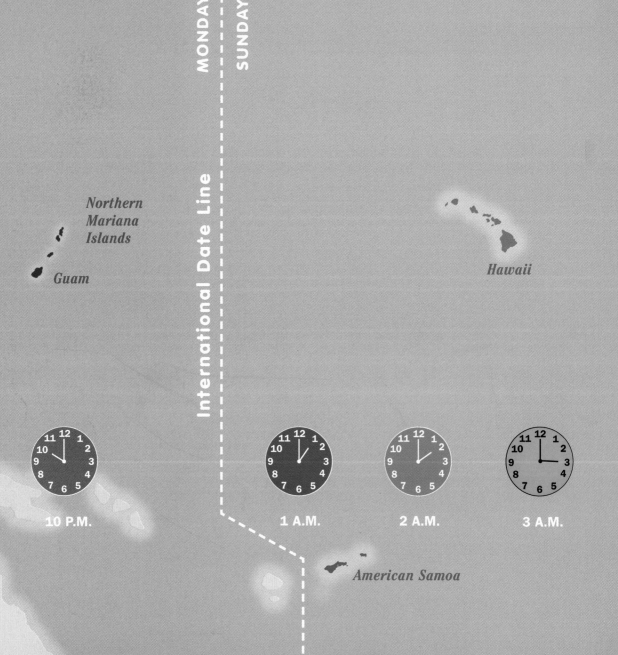

MONDAY
SUNDAY

International Date Line

Northern
Mariana
Islands

Guam

Hawaii

American Samoa

10 P.M.   1 A.M.   2 A.M.   3 A.M.

4 A.M.   5 A.M.   6 A.M.   7 A.M.

Appendices

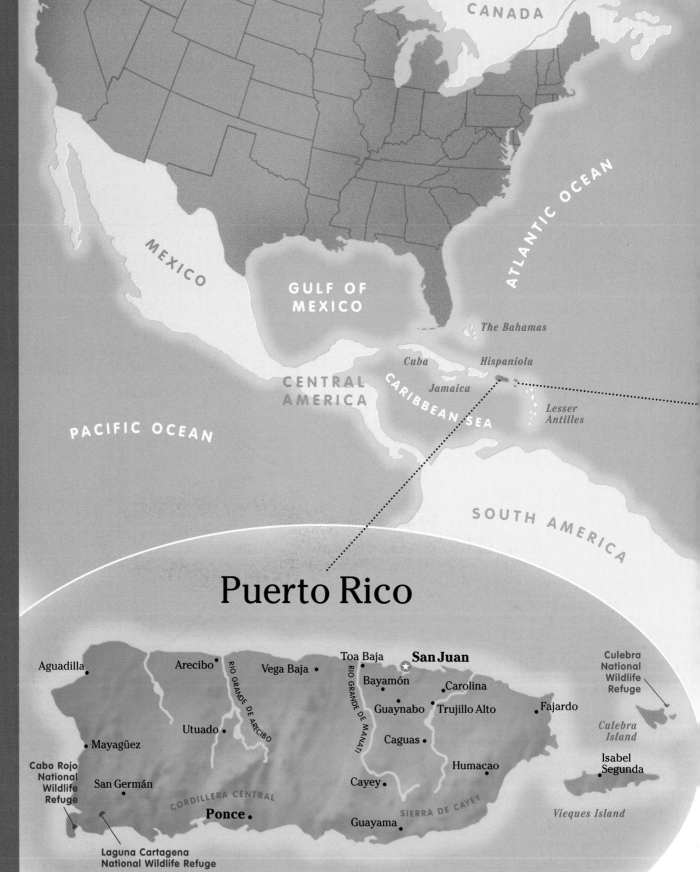

Puerto Rico

CANADA

ATLANTIC OCEAN

MEXICO

GULF OF
MEXICO

The Bahamas

Cuba   *Hispaniola*

CENTRAL
AMERICA

CARIBBEAN SEA   *Jamaica*   *Lesser
Antilles*

PACIFIC OCEAN

SOUTH AMERICA

Aguadilla

Arecibo   Vega Baja   Toa Baja   **San Juan**

RIO GRANDE DE ARECIBO   RIO GRANDE DE MANATI   Bayamón   Carolina

Utuado   Guaynabo   Trujillo Alto   Fajardo

Mayagüez   Caguas

Cabo Rojo
National
Wildlife
Refuge   San Germán   Humacao   Isabel
Segunda

CORDILLERA CENTRAL   Cayey

Ponce   SIERRA DE CAYEY   *Culebra
Island*

Guayama   *Vieques Island*

Culebra
National
Wildlife
Refuge

Laguna Cartagena
National Wildlife Refuge

◄─────────── 112 miles (180 km) ───────────►

Atlantic Possessions

St. Thomas

★ **Charlotte Amalie**

St. John

Virgin Islands National Park

U.S. Virgin Islands

←——— 35 miles (56 km) ———→

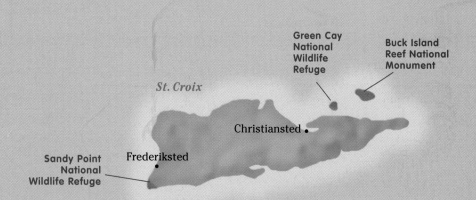

Green Cay National Wildlife Refuge

Buck Island Reef National Monument

St. Croix

Christiansted •

Sandy Point National Wildlife Refuge

Frederiksted •

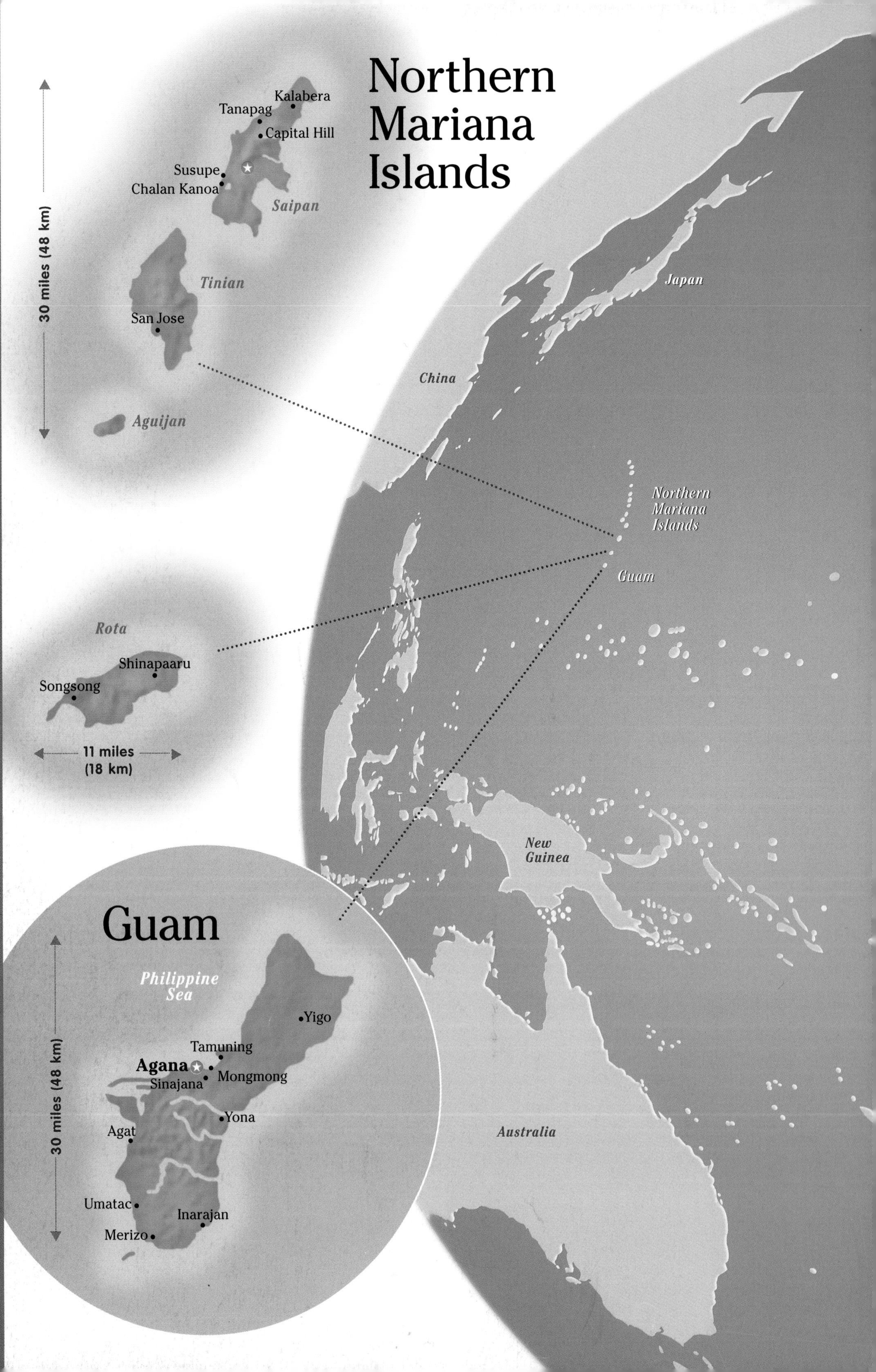

Northern Mariana Islands

Kalabera

Tanapag

Capital Hill

Susupe

Chalan Kanoa

Saipan

Tinian

San Jose

Aguijan

30 miles (48 km)

Rota

Shinapaaru

Songsong

11 miles
(18 km)

Japan

China

*Northern
Mariana
Islands*

Guam

*New
Guinea*

Guam

*Philippine
Sea*

Yigo

Tamuning

Agana

Sinajana

Mongmong

Yona

Agat

30 miles (48 km)

Umatac

Inarajan

Merizo

Australia

Pacific Possessions

Aleutian Islands

PACIFIC OCEAN

Hawaii

American Samoa

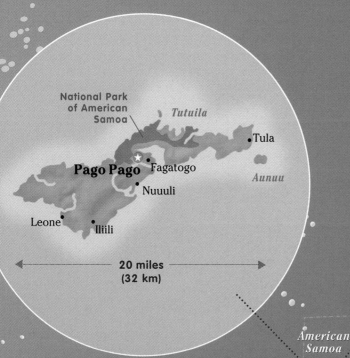

National Park of American Samoa

Tutuila

• Tula

Pago Pago ★

Fagatogo

Nuuuli

Aunuu

Leone •

Iliili •

20 miles
(32 km)

Olosega

Ofu

Tau

• Maia

Tau •

*Manua
Islands*

National Park
of American
Samoa

18 miles
(29 km)

*American
Samoa*

*Western
Samoa*

Fiji

Tonga

U.S. Population Density

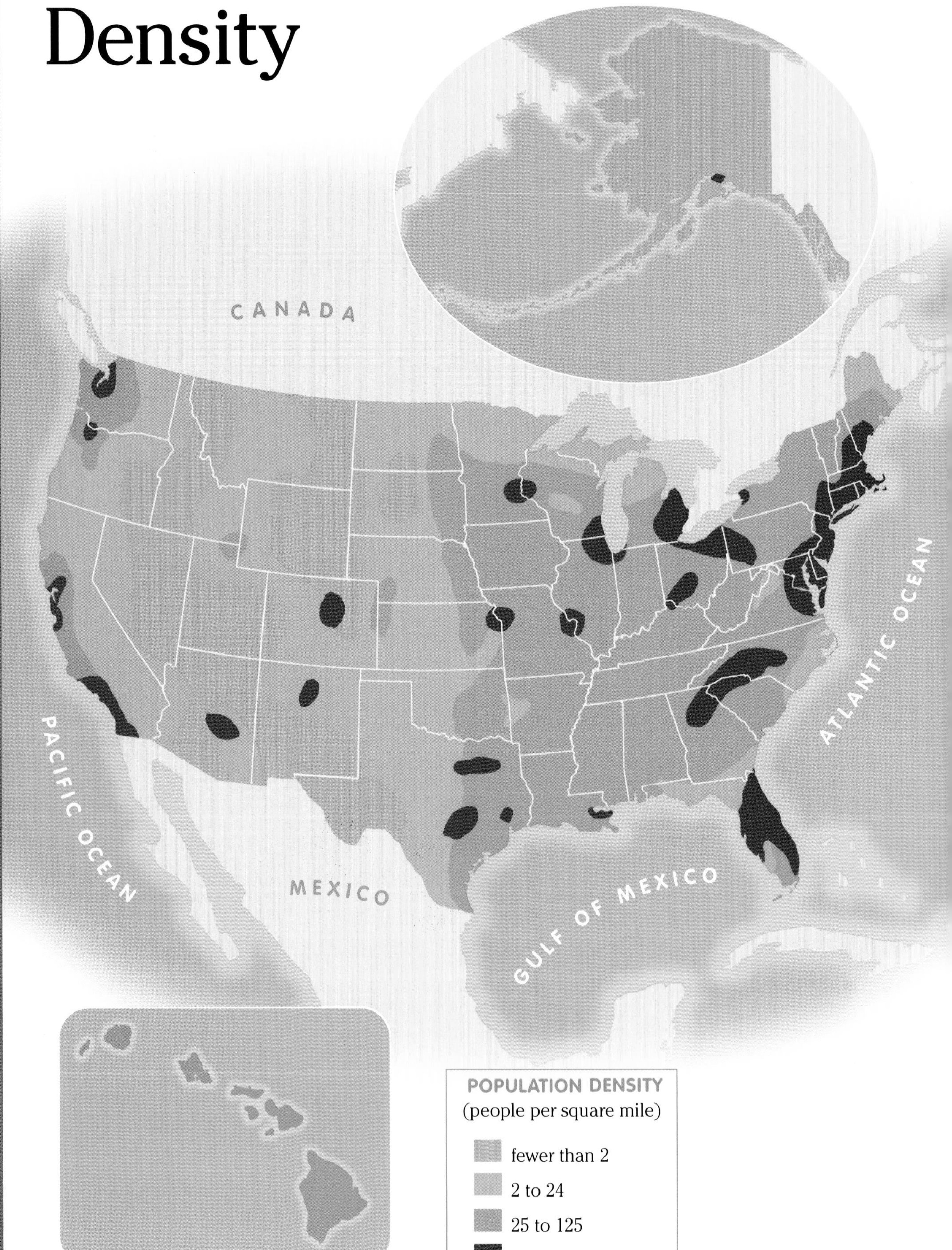

CANADA

PACIFIC OCEAN

MEXICO

GULF OF MEXICO

ATLANTIC OCEAN

POPULATION DENSITY
(people per square mile)

- fewer than 2
- 2 to 24
- 25 to 125
- more than 125

Major U.S. River Systems

CANADA

PACIFIC OCEAN

MEXICO

GULF OF MEXICO

ATLANTIC OCEAN

RIVER SYSTEMS

Colorado

Columbia

Mississippi–Missouri

Rio Grande

Yukon

U.S. Geographic Regions

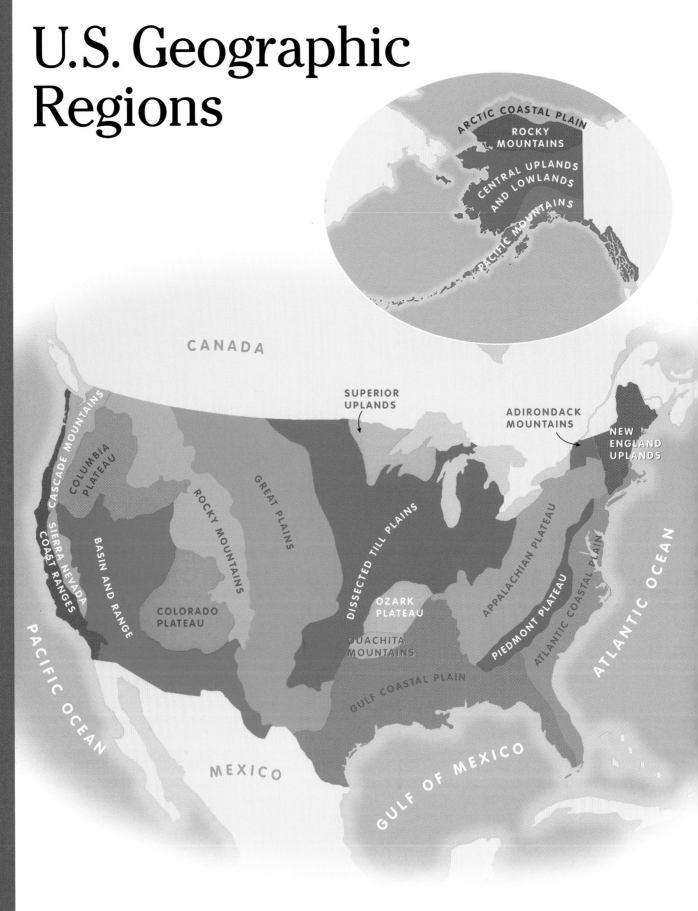

ARCTIC COASTAL PLAIN

ROCKY MOUNTAINS

CENTRAL UPLANDS AND LOWLANDS

PACIFIC MOUNTAINS

CANADA

SUPERIOR UPLANDS

ADIRONDACK MOUNTAINS

NEW ENGLAND UPLANDS

CASCADE MOUNTAINS

COLUMBIA PLATEAU

ROCKY MOUNTAINS

GREAT PLAINS

DISSECTED TILL PLAINS

APPALACHIAN PLATEAU

SIERRA NEVADA COAST RANGES

BASIN AND RANGE

OZARK PLATEAU

PIEDMONT PLATEAU

ATLANTIC COASTAL PLAIN

ATLANTIC OCEAN

COLORADO PLATEAU

OUACHITA MOUNTAINS

PACIFIC OCEAN

GULF COASTAL PLAIN

MEXICO

GULF OF MEXICO

U.S. Territorial Expansion

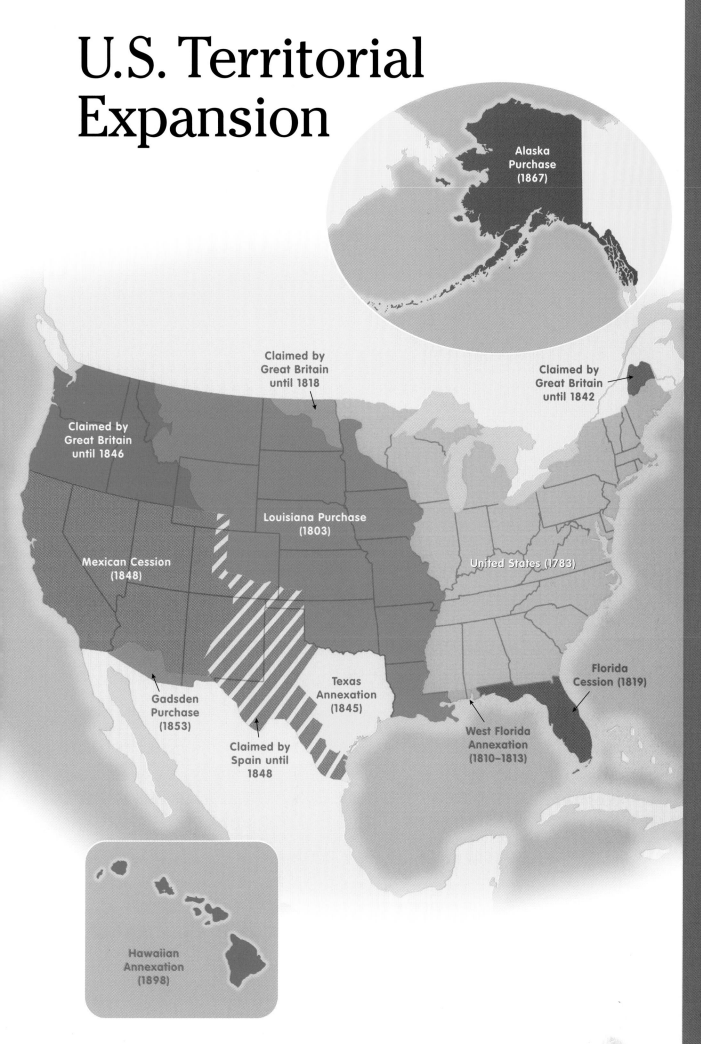

Alaska Purchase (1867)

Claimed by Great Britain until 1818

Claimed by Great Britain until 1842

Claimed by Great Britain until 1846

Louisiana Purchase (1803)

Mexican Cession (1848)

United States (1783)

Gadsden Purchase (1853)

Texas Annexation (1845)

Claimed by Spain until 1848

Florida Cession (1819)

West Florida Annexation (1810–1813)

Hawaiian Annexation (1898)

Glossary

aquifer an underground layer of rock, sand, or gravel that holds water

arable suitable for growing crops

arid excessively dry; also, receiving too little rainfall to support agriculture

atoll a coral island consisting of a reef encircling a lagoon

bald a treeless hilltop

basin a depression in the earth's surface; also, the area drained by a river and its tributaries

bayou a slow-moving creek

bedrock solid rock underlying a surface layer of soil

bluff a high steep bank or cliff

bog an area of wet, spongy ground

bottomland a low-lying region along a waterway

butte an isolated hill or mountain with steep sides (smaller than a mesa)

canal an artificial waterway constructed to aid navigation

canyon a deep narrow valley with steep sides, often with a stream or river flowing through it

channel a narrow passage of sea between two close landmasses

Continental Divide the principal watershed of North America, separating the Atlantic and Pacific ocean basins

continental United States the coterminous landmass of the United States, composed of forty-eight states (excluding Alaska and Hawaii)

crater the bowl-shaped depression atop a volcano

delta the land created by sediment deposits at the mouth of a river

divide a watershed, or dividing ridge between drainage areas

drift debris transported by a glacier

escarpment a cliff or steep slope between two level surfaces

estuary the area in which an ocean tide meets a river current

fall line the line along which a plateau drops abruptly, creating river rapids and waterfalls

fault a fracture in the earth's crust

floodplain level land occasionally submerged by floodwaters

foothills hilly region at the base of a mountain range

front the line defining the base of a mountain range

glaciation the process, or result, of being covered by a glacier

glacier a huge sheet of ice

gorge a narrow canyon

head of navigation the point on a river past which ships cannot travel

kettle lake a steep-sided lake formed by a glacier

levee a raised structure built to keep a river within its channel (and thereby prevent flooding)

loess soil composed of dirt deposited by the wind

mesa an isolated, flat-topped elevation of land (smaller than a plateau)

monadnock an isolated plug of granite that becomes a mountain after the surrounding land erodes away

oxbow lake a curved lake formed when a meandering river takes a more direct course, isolating a bend

peninsula a spit of land bounded on three sides by water

plateau a large, generally flat area rising above the surrounding land on at least one side

prairie mostly level or rolling land characterized by deep fertile soil, plentiful grass, and few trees

precipitation water deposited by clouds in the form of hail, mist, rain, sleet, or snow

rangeland land suitable for grazing livestock

sediment material deposited by water, wind, or glaciers

silt sediment deposited by moving water

subsoil the layer of weathered material underneath the topsoil

tableland broad, level, elevated land, as a plateau

terminal moraine rocky debris deposited at the front edge of a glacier

tidal river a river whose current is periodically affected (or reversed) by the force of ocean tides

tidewater low-lying coastal land characterized by numerous tidal rivers

till glacial drift containing a mixture of clay, sand, gravel, and boulders

topography the physical features of a region of land

topsoil the organic layer of soil closest to the surface into which plants sink their roots

tributary a river or stream that flows into a larger watercourse

tundra a level or rolling treeless plain with a permanently frozen subsoil

watershed a region, bounded by divides, draining into a particular body of water

Index

Adirondack Mountains, 31, 134
Alabama, 38–39
    Black Belt, 39
    black churches, 39
    peanut growing, 38
    Rocket City, U.S.A., 38
Alaska, 19, 31, 48, 89, 95–96, 116–117, 135
    airplane as family "car," 117
    largest state, 117
    Matanuska Valley cabbages, 116
    mountains, 117
    Trans-Alaska Pipeline, 116
Aleutian Islands, 115, 117
All-American Soap Box Derby, 76
Allegheny Mountains, 27, 33, 59, 61, 77
American Samoa, 131
Amish, 33, 76–77
Appalachian Mountains, 9, 33, 37, 39, 47, 53, 59, 61, 91, 134
Appalachian Trail, 12
apple growing, 31, 125
aquaculture, 50, 94
aquifers, 29, 85, 136
Arctic Coastal Plain, 117, 134
Arizona, 103–105
    copper mining, 104
    Grand Canyon, 104–105
    intermittent rivers, 105
    Mexican influences, 105
    Sonoran Desert, 105
Arkansas, 40–41, 51
    chicken raising, 40
    Hot Springs, 41
    Ozark Folk Center, 41
    Ozark Mountains, 41
Arkansas River, 41, 91
Atlantic Coastal Plain, 15, 19, 23, 27, 33, 37, 45, 53, 55, 59, 134
automobile manufacturing, 47, 57, 70, 74
Basin and Range, 105, 109, 134
bats, 109, 112
bayous, 49, 136
Beech, Walter, 82

beef cattle raising, 83, 85, 89, 93, 97, 101, 107, 109, 111–113
Block, Adriaen, 19
Blue Ridge Mountains, 45, 53, 55, 59
bluegrass music, 47
blues music, 65
Cajuns, 49
California, 48, 77, 79, 85, 93, 100, 103, 107, 113, 118–119, 123
    Central Valley farming, 118
    Coast Ranges, 119
    cuisine, 119
    highest and lowest points in U.S., 118
    San Andreas Fault, 119
Cascade Mountains, 119, 123, 125, 134
Cavelier, Robert, 49
caves, 47, 109
Central Uplands and Lowlands (Alaska), 134
Charles I (king of England), 27, 53, 55
chemical manufacturing, 29, 49, 57, 113
Chesapeake Bay, 25, 27, 58–59
Chesapeake Bay Bridge-Tunnel, 59
chicken raising, 25, 27, 40
chinook winds, 97
Church of Jesus Christ of Latter-day Saints
    see Mormons
citrus growing, 43, 99, 113
Civil War, 39, 47, 55, 57, 59, 61, 77
coal mining, 33, 46–47, 60–61, 67, 96–97, 100–101, 109
Coast Ranges, 115, 119, 123, 134
Cohansey Aquifer, 29
Colonial Williamsburg, 59
Colorado, 92–93
    elevation, 93
    defense industry, 92
    Denver as capital of Mountain West, 93
    ski resorts, 93
Colorado Plateau, 93, 99, 105, 109, 134
Colorado River, 91, 93, 103, 105, 107, 119, 133
Colt, Samuel, 11
Columbia Plateau, 95, 123, 125, 134
Columbia River, 123–125, 133

Columbus, Christopher, 35
Connecticut, 10–11, 17
    Fairfield County wealth, 11
    gaming, Native American, 11
    insurance industry in Hartford, 10
    tobacco leaf, shade-grown, 11
    weather, 10
Connecticut River, 9, 11, 15, 21
Connecticut Yankee in King Arthur's Court
   (Twain), 11
Continental Divide, 91, 97, 101, 136
copper mining, 97, 104, 109
Corn Belt, 75, 77
corn growing, 85, 89
cotton growing, 39, 41, 45, 49–50, 55, 111
country music, 57, 113
Crater Lake, 123
Crater of Diamonds State Park, 40
Creole, 49
cuisine, 49, 71, 119
Cumberland Mountains, 47, 56–57
dairy industry, 21, 31–33, 73, 79
Delaware, 24–25
    Chateau Country, 25
    chemical manufacturing, 24–25
    rounded border, 25
    shoreline protection laws, 25
Delmarva Peninsula, 25
Dexter Avenue Baptist Church, 39
Dissected Till Plains, 63, 65, 77, 83, 85, 134
District of Columbia *see* Washington, D.C.
drift, 79, 87, 136
Drift Prairie, 87, 89
Driftless Area, 79
Du Pont, 24–25
Dust Bowl, 111
earthquakes, 115, 119
Edison, Thomas, 29
Elizabeth I (queen of England), 59
Empire State Building, 67
Emporia Gazette, 83
endangered species, 95, 123
environmental protection laws, 25, 79, 122
Everglades, 43
fall line, 23, 136
Faulkner, William, 51
federal government, as employer, 27, 34–35,
   59, 121
Florida, 42–43, 135
    citrus growing, 43

    Everglades, 43
    Hispanic influences, 43
    tourism, 42–43
food processing, 27, 33, 68, 87, 96 *(see also*
   meatpacking)
football, 33, 85
Four Corners, 108
Franklin, Benjamin, 29
French Canadians, 12, 15, 19, 49
Frost, Robert, 21
Fyr Bal Festival, 79
Gadsden Purchase, 135
gambling, 11, 106–107
geographic regions, U.S., 134
George II (king of England), 45
Georgia, 44–45
    Atlanta as capital of New South, 45
    carpet making, 45
    red clay hills, 45
    Savannah Landmark District, 44
Glacier National Park, 97
glaciers, 13, 15, 31, 63, 65, 67, 69, 73, 75, 77,
   79, 87, 89, 137
gold, 97, 99, 104, 107
Goodyear, Charles, 11
Grand Canyon, 104–105, 109
Grand Ole Opry, 57
Great American Desert, 85
Great Basin, 95, 99, 103, 107
Great Dismal Swamp, 53
Great Lakes, 31, 33, 64–65, 71 *(see also*
   individual lakes)
Great Plains, 75, 81, 83, 85, 87, 89, 93, 97, 101,
   109, 134
Great Smoky Mountains, 53, 57
Green Mountains, 9, 21
Guam, 130
Gulf Coastal Plain, 45, 113, 134
Gullah, 55
Hawaii, 120–121, 135
    Mauna Kea, 121
    pineapple growing, 120
    "shaka" sign, 121
    snowfall, 120
    volcanic beaches, 121
Hawaiian Trough, 121
Henrietta Maria (queen of England), 27
Hershey, Milton, 32
High Lava Plains, 123
High Plains, 93, 111, 113

High Plains Aquifer, 85
high-tech industries, 15, 53, 69, 112, 123, 125
Hoover Dam, 107
hydroelectric power, 57, 124
Ice Age, 27, 31, 63, 65, 67, 73, 79, 87
Idaho, 94–95
    aquaculture, 94
    Hells Canyon, 94
    Mormon population, 95
    wilderness areas, 95
    World Center for Birds of Prey, 95
Illinois, 64–65, 67, 79
    blues music, 65
    glaciation, 65
    skyscrapers, 65
    transportation system, 64–65
Indiana, 66–67
    deforestation, 67
    Hoosier, origin of, 66
    Hoosier Hysteria, 67
    limestone quarries, 67
    steel industry in Gary, 66–67
Inside Passage, 117
insurance industry, 10, 69, 84, 99
Intermontane Basin, 101
Iowa, 67–69, 73, 79
    agricultural employment, 68
    cultural life, 69
    high school graduation rate, 68
    small towns, 69
    uniformity, 69
Iowa Writers' Workshop, 69
irrigation, 85, 125
Jackson, Andrew, 47
Jacob's Pillow Dance Festival, 14
James II (king of England), 31
jazz music, 49, 113
Jefferson, Thomas, 59
Kansas, 82–83, 85, 86, 111
    geographic center of continental U.S., 83
    light aircraft manufacturing, 82
    newspapers, 82–83
    wheat growing, 83
Keillor, Garrison, 73
Kentucky, 46–47
    bluegrass music, 47
    coal mining, 46–47
    Mammoth Cave National Park, 47
    racehorses, 47
Kentucky Derby, 47, 79

kettle lakes, 67, 137
King, Martin Luther, Jr., 39, 45
Klamath Mountains, 119
Lake Bonneville, 99
Lake Erie, 77
Lake Huron, 71
Lake Michigan, 71
Lake Superior, 70–71, 73
León, Juan Ponce de, 43
Levinson, Barry, 27
Lincoln, Abraham, 65
loess, 69, 137
Longfellow Mountains, 9
Los Alamos National Laboratory, 108–109
Louis XIV (king of France), 49
Louisiana, 48–49, 51, 100
    bayous, 49
    cuisine, 49
    levees in New Orleans, 49
    oil and gas exploration, offshore, 48
    parishes, 48
Louisiana Purchase, 135
lumber industry *see* timber industry
Maine, 12–13
    French as primary language, 12
    lobster industry, 13
    Mount Katahdin, sunrise on, 12
    potato growing in Aroostook County, 13
    shoreline, 13
Mammoth Cave National Park, 47
Mankiller, Wilma, 111
Marshall Space Flight Center, 38
Maryland, 26–27
    Chesapeake Bay, changing shoreline, 27
    filmmaking, 27
    Oriole Park at Camden Yards, 26
    seafood industry, 27
Mason, Captain John, 17
Massachusetts, 14–15
    Berkshires, music and dance in, 14
    Cape Cod as terminal moraine, 15
    cranberry bogs, 15
    Route 128 technology firms, 15
meatpacking, 68, 84
Mennonites, 33, 83
Mesabi Range, 72–73
Mexican Cession, 135
Michigan, 70–71
    automobile manufacturing, 70
    cherry growing, 71

fish boils, 71
shipping, Great Lakes, 71
mining, 72–73, 93, 95, 97, 99–101, 104, 106–107,
   109 (see also coal mining, copper mining,
   gold mining, silver mining)
Minnesota, 67, 71–73, 79
   iron ore mining, 72
   lake names, 72
   Mississippi River, source of, 73
   Prairie Home Companion, A, 73
   watersheds, 73
Miss America pageant, 29
Mississippi, 50–51
   catfish farms, 50
   Faulkner Country, 51
   Mississippi Delta topsoil, 50–51
   oxbow lakes, 51
Mississippi River, 37, 49–51, 56, 64–65, 69, 73,
   75, 133
Missouri, 74–75
   Big Spring, 75
   Gateway Arch, 75
   Show Me State, 75
   transportation equipment manufacturing,
   74
Missouri Plateau, 87
Missouri River, 69, 75, 89, 91, 133
Mogollon Rim, 105
monadnocks, 17, 137
Monroe, Bill, 47
Montana, 96–97, 101
   chinook winds, 97
   outdoor lifestyle, 97
   remoteness of western Montana, 97
   wood-related products, 96
Mormons, 95, 98–99
Mount Everest, 121
Mount Rushmore, 89
Mount St. Helens, 115, 125
"mountain music," 61
Mountain Stage, 61
music, 47, 49, 57, 61, 65, 113
Native American gaming, 11
Nebraska, 77, 84–85
   Huskermania, 85
   irrigation, 85
   meatpacking, 84
   surveyed using grid system, 85
Nevada, 99, 104, 105–107
   arid climate, 107

Extraterrestrial Highway, 107
fastest-growing state, 107
gambling, 106–107
marriage laws and weddings, 106–107
New England Uplands, 9, 15, 19, 134
New Hampshire, 16–17
   Manchester, manufacturing in, 16
   Mount Washington winds, 17
   presidential primary, "first in the
      nation," 17
   town meetings, 17
New Jersey, 18, 28–29
   Jersey Shore, 29
   population density, 29
   transportation system, 28
   truck farming, 29
New Mexico, 89, 108–109
   Carlsbad Caverns, 109
   elevation, 109
   Four Corners, 108
   Los Alamos National Laboratory, 108–109
   Pueblo pottery, 109
New York, 30–31, 119
   Hudson River Valley, 31
   lake-effect snow, 31
   racial and ethnic diversity, 31
   Wall Street, 30–31
New York Stock Exchange, 30
North American Aerospace Defense
   Command (NORAD), 92
North American Plate, 115, 119
North Carolina, 45, 47, 52–53
   Cherokee population, 53
   Outer Banks, 53
   Research Triangle Park, 53
   tobacco farming, 52–53
North Dakota, 86–87
   bookmobiles, 87
   forested land, lack of, 87
   stepped plateaus, 87
   wheat growing, 86
Northern Mariana Islands, 130
Oak Ridge National Laboratory, 56
Ogallala Aquifer, 85
Oglethorpe, James, 44–45
Ohio, 76–77
   Amish, 76–77
   Corn Belt, 77
   pollution, Lake Erie, 77
   tire industry in Akron, 76

Ohio River, 33, 47, 61, 77
oil and gas industry, 48–49, 51, 96–97,
100–101, 109–113, 116–117
Okefenokee Swamp, 45
Oklahoma, 110–111
    climate, 111
    Native American population, 111
    oil and gas industry, 110–111
    Red River Valley, 111
    tornadoes, 110–111
Oregon, 122–123
    Albany Timber Carnival, 122
    bicycles, free in Portland, 123
    Crater Lake, 123
    environmental protection laws, 122
    Willamette River Valley, 123
Oregon Trail, 84–85
Ouachita Mountains, 41, 111, 134
oxbow lakes, 51, 137
Ozark Folk Center, 41
Ozark Mountains, 41, 75, 111, 134
O'Keeffe, Georgia, 109
Pacific Mountains, 134
Pacific Plate, 115, 119
peanut growing, 38, 45, 111
Pearl Harbor, 121
Penn, Sir William (father of the Quaker
  leader), 33
Penn, William, 25, 33
Pennsylvania, 25, 32–33, 77
    Hershey chocolate factory, 32
    hunting, 33
    Pennsylvania Dutch, 32–33
    steel industry, 32–33
Pentagon, 58, 67
petroleum industry *see* oil and gas industry
Piedmont Plateau, 23, 27, 33, 37, 45, 53, 55,
  59, 134
Platte River, 85, 91
pollution, 25, 27, 29, 46, 66, 77, 105, 117
 123
population density, 13, 18, 29, 89, 97, 132
potato growing, 13, 95
Prairie Home Companion, A, 73
Puerto Rico, 128
Raleigh, Walter, 59
Red River, 87, 111
Research Triangle Park, 53
Rhode Island, 18–19, 112
    costume jewelry manufacturing , 19

    Newport Cliff Walk, 18
    population density, 18
    smallest state, 19
    yachting in Narragansett Bay, 19
Ring of Fire, 115
Rio Grande, 91, 109, 113, 133
river systems, major U.S., 133
rocketry, 38, 98
Rocky Mountains, 91, 93, 95, 97, 99, 101, 103,
  109, 134
Rogers, Will, 109
St. Lawrence Seaway, 71
San Andreas Fault, 119
Sandia National Laboratories, 108
Sears Tower, 65
shipping, 49, 57, 64–65, 71, 73, 75, 77, 113
Sierra Nevada, 107, 119, 134
Silicon Valley, 15, 125
silver mining, 97, 99, 104, 107
skiing, 20, 93
small-town way of life, 21, 69, 83
Smith, Captain John, 15
Snake River, 95, 124
South Carolina, 54–55
    coastline, 55
    Grand Strand, 55
    Sea Islands, 55
    Textile Belt, 54
South Dakota, 88–89
    Black Hills, 89
    buffalo, free-roaming, 88
    credit-card processing in Sioux Falls, 88
    Native American cultural heritage, 89
    tourism, 89
Springsteen, Bruce, 29
steel industry, 32–33, 39, 66–67, 77
Sun Belt, 105
Superior Uplands, 134
Susquehanna River, 27
Syttende Mai, 79
Tanglewood, 14
Tejano music, 113
Tennessee, 56–57
    country music, 57
    Great Smoky Mountains, 57
    Oak Ridge National Laboratory, 56
    Reelfoot Lake, 56
    Tennessee Valley Authority (TVA), 57
Tennessee River, 57
Tennessee Valley Authority (TVA), 57

terminal moraine, 15, 137

territorial expansion, U.S., 135

Texas, 29, 48, 77, 85, 100, 109, 111–113, 135

    Austin music clubs, 113

    King Ranch, 112

    streets and highways, 113

    wildflowers, 113

textile manufacturing, 15, 45, 53–54

Tidewater, 53, 59, 137

till, 63, 67, 137

timber industry, 13, 17, 39, 71, 79, 95–96, 119,
    122–123, 125

tobacco farming, 11, 47, 52–53, 55

tornadoes, 81, 110–111

tourism, 13, 34, 41–43, 89, 95, 99, 101, 106, 121

transportation equipment manufacturing,
    11, 57, 74, 82 *(see also* automobile
    manufacturing)

transportation industry, 28, 64–65, 75
    (see also shipping)

Truman, Harry, 75

Twain, Mark, 10–11

U.S. Virgin Islands, 129

Utah, 98–99

    Great Salt Lake, 99

    Monument Valley, 99

    Mormon population, 98–99

    rocketry, 98

Vandiver, Willard D., 75

Vermont, 20–21

    covered bridges, 20

    dairy industry, 21

    ski resorts, 20

    small towns, 21

    sugaring, 21

Verrazano, Giovanni da, 19

Virginia, 58–59

    Chesapeake Bay Bridge–Tunnel, 59

    historic sites, 59

    naval bases, 58–59

    Shenandoah Valley, 59

volcanoes, 115, 121, 123, 125

Walt Disney World, 42

Wasatch Mountains, 91, 99

Washington, 117, 123–125

    Grand Coulee Dam, 124

    Mount St. Helens, 125

    rain shadow of Cascade Mountains, 125

    San Juan Islands, 124–125

    wildlife watching, 125

Washington, D.C., 23, 34–35, 59

    federal government, as employer, 34–35

    land grant, 35

    lawyers, 34

    tourism, 34–35

    urban problems, 35

Washington, George, 23, 35, 59, 125

Waters, Alice, 119

Waters, John, 27

Welty, Eudora, 51

West, Thomas, 25

West Virginia, 33, 47, 60–61

    coal mining, 60–61

    "mountain music," 61

    population decline, 61

    Spruce Knob, 61

wheat growing, 83, 85–86, 89, 97, 111

White, William Allen, 83

White Mountains, 9, 15, 17

William Tell Festival, 79

Williams, Tennessee, 51

wind, 17, 97

Winterthur, 25

Wisconsin, 78–79

    breweries in Milwaukee, 78

    dairy industry, 79

    North Woods, 79

    Oshkosh Fly–In, 79

    toilet paper manufacturing, 78

Wyoming, 47, 60, 100–101

    federal ownership of land, 101

    Frontier Days, 101

    oil and gas industry, 100–101

    rangeland, 101

Yale, Linus, 11

Yankees, 11, 15, 21

Young, Brigham, 99

Yukon Plateau, 117

Yukon River, 133

zydeco music, 49

Photo Credits